CASE STUDIES IN
CULTURAL ANTHROPOLOGY

GENERAL EDITORS

George and Louise Spindler

STANFORD UNIVERSITY

GRAND VALLEY DANI

Peaceful Warriors

Second Edition

GRAND VALLEY DANI
Peaceful Warriors

Second Edition

KARL G. HEIDER

University of South Carolina

HOLT, RINEHART AND WINSTON, INC.
FORT WORTH   CHICAGO   SAN FRANCISCO   PHILADELPHIA
MONTREAL   TORONTO   LONDON   SYDNEY   TOKYO

Publisher   Ted Buchholz
Acquisitions Editor   Chris Klein
Project Editor   Catherine Townsend
Production Manager   Kathleen Ferguson
Art & Design Supervisor   John Ritland
Cover Designer   Vicki McAlindon Horton
Compositor   Publications Development Co.

Library of Congress Cataloging-in-Publication Data

Heider, Karl G., 1935–
    Grand Valley Dani, peaceful warriors / Karl G. Heider — 2nd ed.
       p.   cm. — (Case studies in cultural anthropology)
    Includes bibliographical references and index.
    ISBN 0-03-052553-5 (paperback)
    1. Dani (New Guinea people)   I. Title.   II. Title: Peaceful
warriors.   III. Series.
DU744.35.D32H44   1990
995.1—dc20   90-41384
                                                  CIP

ISBN: 0-03-052553-5

Address Orders to: 6277 Sea Harbor Drive, Orlando, FL 32887 1-800-782-4479, or 1-800-433-0001 (in Florida)

Address Editorial Correspondence to: 301 Commerce Street, Suite 3700, Fort Worth, TX 76102

Printed in the United States of America

1 2 3 4 016   20 19 18 17 16 15

Holt, Rinehart and Winston, Inc.
The Dryden Press
Saunders College Publishing

Foreword

ABOUT THE SERIES

These case studies in cultural anthropology are designed to bring to students, in beginning and intermediate courses in the social sciences, insights into the richness and complexity of human life as it is lived in different ways and in different places. They are written by men and women who have lived in the societies they write about and who are professionally trained as observers and interpreters of human behavior. The authors are also teachers, and in writing their books they have kept the students who will read them foremost in their minds. It is our belief that when an understanding of ways of life very different from one's own is gained, abstractions and generalizations about social structure, cultural values, subsistence techniques, and the other universal categories of human social behavior become meaningful.

ABOUT THE AUTHOR

Karl G. Heider was born in Northampton, Massachusetts, and went to high school in Lawrence, Kansas. In 1952 he spent the summer between high school and college as a shovel hand on an archaeological dig in South Dakota. He has been in anthropology ever since. After digging for two more summers in South Dakota, he did a brief ethnography of the Fort McDowell Yavapai in Arizona for his honors thesis at Harvard. Then, after graduating in 1956, he spent a year wandering through Asia on a Sheldon Traveling Fellowship. He did some archaeology on the Kwae Noi River in Thailand, was in the film *Bridge on the River Kwai,* and generally visited everywhere he could. The next year he studied ethnology at the University of Vienna, and then returned to Harvard for his M.A. (1959) and Ph.D. (1966) in anthropology. In 1960 while digging at the Mayan site of Tikal in Guatemala, he made his first film, *Tikal.* In 1961 he joined the Harvard–Peabody Expedition in New Guinea and began the study of the Grand Valley Dani who are described here. After finishing his Ph.D., he taught at Harvard for a year and then at Brown University for four years. Then he moved to California where he taught at the University of California, Berkeley, at Stanford, and at UCLA, and was a Fellow at the Center for Advanced Study in the Behavioral Sciences. In 1975 he moved to the University of South Carolina to be the first chairman of the new Department of Anthropology there. Recently, he has carried out two years of fieldwork among the Minangkabau of West Sumatra, Indonesia, on the cultural patterning of emotion. He is also working on a cultural analysis of Indonesian cinema.

ABOUT THIS CASE STUDY

In this case study Karl Heider has condensed many of the most important observations and interpretations issuing from his long and productive engagement with the Dugum Dani of the Grand Valley of the Balim River in the central highlands of Irian/New Guinea. The approach is unusual in the range of topics covered and in the succinctness with which they are covered, and also because the author introduces us to the Dani by telling us about his fieldwork, his ethical dilemmas, and the circumstances of his contact with the Dani. One immediately acquires a sense of the limitations and strengths of the anthropological role in the field situation. The Dani become not less, but more real to the reader, as one approaches them and their culture through the experience of a fellow Westerner. One has a bit of the feeling of what it would be like to have been in Heider's place, seeing with his eyes.

This case study is also notable for the author's willingness to admit not having explanations for certain phenomena and to encourage further study to expand our knowledge of the Dani. All too often we gain the feeling as we read ethnographies that the author has mastered the native language perfectly (which is rarely the case) and knows the culture much better than any native member of the society in which the anthropologist is a resident guest. No anthropologist, in fact, ever masters the native language or comes to know all aspects of the culture thoroughly.

It is fortunate that the very well-known film, *Dead Birds,* is available for use with this case study, as well as the other films shot by Heider himself. This combination of films and case study makes an unbeatable instructional unit.

GEORGE AND LOUISE SPINDLER
Series Editors
Calistoga, California

ABOUT THIS NEW EDITION

What we said above about Karl Heider's writings on the Dani in the "ethnographic present" of the 1960s still holds good. Now, we have a glimpse of the Dani in 1988. It is good to know that the Dani are not being wiped out. It is good to know that their environment is not being destroyed, that their land is still productive, and in fact that its productivity has been enhanced by the introduction of new plants and methods of horticulture. In brief, it is good to know that the Dani are not, or at least not yet, experiencing the genocidal shock that frequently accompanies the entrance of the outside world into the domains of tribal peoples. When the "outside world," dominated by technology and material culture originating from the West, breaks in on a tribal people, as it has everywhere in the world by now, the long-range results are usually disastrous, if traditional tribal culture and society are taken as the baseline to compare such change. Social disorganization and deculturation have become unpopular terms of late, but they do describe the process of "adaptation," in part at least. But, of course, more is happening, and in the case of the Dugum Dani the "more" is as clear as the loss. A bifurcated population has emerged. One speaks Indonesian, has been to school, and looks to the wider world. The other speaks only Dani, has not been to school, and is locked into a deteriorating traditional culture.

A longer time in the field would yield answers about how this bifurcated population mediates its internal relationships, about how and in what specific ways the traditional Dani culture persists in the new generation (for surely it does), and about how the Dani will make their way further into the new world that has begun to occupy their space and to transform them. We are grateful to Karl Heider for this informative look at what is happening.

GEORGE AND LOUISE SPINDLER
Series Editors
Calistoga, California

ACKNOWLEDGMENTS

I am greatly indebted to many Dani for their patience and good humor. In particular, I would like to mention Um'ue, his daughter Hagigake, and the other people of the Dugum Neighborhood. Robert Gardner's splendid vision, coupled with his organizing talents, got the Harvard–Peabody Expedition underway. Denise O'Brien and Eleanor Rosch, who also studied the Dani, gave me much help and inspiration, as did Myron Bromley, who knows the Dani better than any of us. Father Frans Verheijen OFM and Father Jules Camps OFM were gracious hosts at Jibiga in 1968 and 1970. I received generous support from many others in the governments of Netherlands New Guinea, the United Nations Temporary Executive Authority, and the Republic of Indonesia; and from among the missionaries of the Order of St. Francis, the Christian and Missionary Association, the Regions Beyond Missionary Union, and the Missionary Fellowship. My research in the field was mainly supported by grants from the National Science Foundation, the Cross-Cultural Study of Ethnocentrism Project, and the Foundations' Fund for Research in Psychiatry, none of whom are responsible for these results. I worked out much of this while a Fellow at the Center for Advanced Study in the Behavioral Sciences at Stanford, California, and did the final writing at the University of South Carolina, where Dean Chester W. Bain of the College of Humanities and Social Sciences helped me get precious time, and Dorothy O'Dell Tart did the typing. Finally, I owe a special debt to the encouragement and interest shown by countless students, friends, and relations who have listened to me talk about the Dani over the past years and who, through their questions and thinking, have helped me to develop these understandings about the Dani.

K. G. H.

ACKNOWLEDGMENTS FOR THE SECOND EDITION

Again, I want to thank Um'ue and his daughter Hagigake for their friendship and hospitality. My 1988 trip to the Grand Valley was made while I was on sabbatical leave from the University of South Carolina and was supported by a generous grant from the Wenner-Gren Foundation for Anthropological Research. I want to acknowledge helpful comments on the first edition from Simon J. Carmel and another colleague whose name, unfortunately, I have misplaced. I dedicate this second edition to Malie Bruton Heider.

K. G. H.

Pronunciation

A few Dani words and names are used here when necessary. For those readers who want to get close to the Dani pronunciation, the following will be of help. The Dani did not have a writing system, so over the years several missionary linguists developed an orthography (see van der Stap 1966:3). The pronunciations are fairly similar to English except in a few cases where Dani phonemes behave differently from the nearest English ones. Most words have equal stress on each syllable. Every vowel is pronounced.

t   This phoneme in a final position is pronounced like the stop "t," but when it occurs between two vowels, it is more like a flapped "r." Thus:

    Mogat (ghost) is mo-gat, but

    Gutelu (the man and the Alliance) is goo-re-loo

k   This phoneme, when it is final, is pronounced like the stop "k," but when it occurs between two vowels, it is a velar fricative, a very soft "g," or it disappears.

    eak (a kinship term) is āyak, but

    jokoik (the bird) is yō-ōyk

j   is the Dutch "j," the English "y"

a   pronounced "ah" (as in "father")—*wa* is wah

i   pronounced ee (as in "see")

    Dani is dah-nee

    wim (war) is weem

    Balim (the river) is bah-leem

e   pronounced "eh" (or as in "bed")

o   pronounced as long "o" (as in "so")

u   pronounced as "oo" (as in "moo")

diphthongs: *ai* (as "eye")

          so *edai-egen* is eh-dye-eh-ken

          oi (as in "boy")

Contents

Introduction

Hidden away in the central mountain ranges of New Guinea a mile above the coastal jungles, the Balim River flows through a broad temperate plain called the "Grand Valley." The valley floor is densely populated by some 50,000 Dani. In the 1960s, the same decade when most of the world watched a man walk on the moon, the Grand Valley Dani still raised their sweet potatoes with fire-hardened digging sticks, made houses for themselves and their pigs with stone adzes, and fought wars with wooden spears and featherless arrows.

The material aspects of Dani culture offered one of our last chances on this planet to see how a horticultural society with the simplest of tools has adapted to its environment.

But behind the external facts of Dani culture lie the complexities of a moiety-based kinship system; a political organization of confederations and alliances of great size but little power; and in the psychological realm, such traits as a five-year postpartum sexual abstinence without stress, a counting system which goes up to three, and tremendous conservatism in the face of great pressures to change their way of life.

New Guinea

A great land mass 1500 miles long and 400 miles wide. Because it is not quite big enough to be called a continent, it is usually termed the second largest island in the world (after Greenland). It lies between Australia and the Equator, where Southeast Asia reaches into the South Pacific. There are two worlds in New Guinea. Around the coast are the lowlands, swamps, jungles, and great meandering rivers. The central core of the island is mountainous, containing the highest mountains between the Himalayas and the Andes, and in a few places there are even glaciers. In 1526 the Portuguese explorer Meneses was the first European to see New Guinea. Europeans soon called it by an African name because of the black-skinned peoples of the coast.

Traditionally, anthropologists speak of two main groups of cultures: the coastal Melanesians and the highland Papuans. The Melanesians speak Austronesian languages related to Polynesian, Micronesian, and Indonesian languages. The Papuans speak non-Austronesian languages. The Papuans are the descendants of the earlier inhabitants of New Guinea who had been pushed into their mountain fastness by later migrations of Melanesians.

1

Papuan

A popular cultural, linguistic, and racial term for the hundreds of thousands of people living in the central highlands of New Guinea, including the Dani, the Kapauku (or Ekagi), and the Gururumba. The Papuan cultures are concentrated in the temperate mountain valley systems between 4000 and 6000 feet (1200–1800 m) altitude. Papuans raise pigs and sweet potatoes, are patrilineal, and, until the last decade or two, have had endemic warfare and used stone tools. Most parts of the highlands have been isolated from world events until recently. Major European contact began only after the Second World War, and intensive anthropological research dates only from the late 1950s and 1960s.

Dani

A general term for a group of closely related Papuan cultures and languages in West New Guinea, including the Jalé (or Eastern Dani), the Western Dani, the Southern Dani, and the centrally located Grand Valley Dani. There may be 200,000 Dani speakers in all. The half-dozen languages and dialects of the Greater Dani Language Family are related to other Non-Austronesian language families of the Irian Jaya Highlands Stock which is in turn in the Trans-New Guinea Phylum. Although some Dani were contacted by European expeditions just before and after World War I, continuous outside contact did not begin until the 1950s.

Grand Valley Dani

About 50,000 Dani live in the Grand Valley of the Balim River, at about latitude 4° south and longitude 138°50′ east. The Grand Valley was probably discovered by Dani centuries ago, but Europeans first found it in 1938, and the first permanent European residents arrived in 1954.

The Dugum Neighborhood

Where some 350 Grand Valley Dani live; it is the main focus of this study and the location of the film *Dead Birds*.

READING THE BOOK

The book begins with two chapters which tell about the fieldwork in New Guinea and about the different attempts which I made to understand the Dani. Study of the Dani proper begins on page 25. Some readers may want to begin there. Some may want to start by flipping through the illustrations to see what the Dani and their land look like.

1 / Studying the Dani

This book is the result of two adventures. The first is a physical adventure: doing fieldwork with the Grand Valley Dani in the central highlands of West New Guinea. The second is a mental adventure which has taken place in the United States as well as in New Guinea: the process of working out an understanding of the Dani.

The fieldwork is finite, with beginning and end marked by stamps in my passport. The process of understanding the Dani has no end, in part because of the tremendous complexity of even an apparently simple Stone Age culture and in part because the questions keep changing. I first went to live with the Dani in 1961. This book tells of my understanding of them 16 years later, in the summer of 1977. Eventually, when more anthropologists have lived with the Dani and thought about the Dani, we should have more and perhaps different understandings of their culture. And someday we might realize that old anthropologists' dream when a Dani comes to tell us about our own culture.

ADVENTURE ONE: THE FIELDWORK

In 1961 when I first met the Dani, the mountains of Netherlands New Guinea were at a moment of maximum culture contrast. It was a sort of time warp. Christian missionaries had built airstrips for small planes in the midst of many people who still had a Stone Age economy. It was a far cry indeed from the conditions which explorers had to face in the eighteenth and nineteenth centuries and even well into the preaviation era of the twentieth century. By the 1960s one could take an international KLM jet flight to Biak in New Guinea; then a two-engine DC-3, that workhorse of World War II, along the coast to Sentani, the airport of the capital, a town then called "Hollandia"; in Sentani, one would board another DC-3 or a small missionary plane for the flight inland, over the coastal swamps, and through the mountain passes to Wamena, a little collection of prefabricated houses which was already becoming the administrative center for the Grand Valley. From Wamena, it was only three or four hours by boat and by foot across the Grand Valley to the Dugum Neighborhood where we settled.

3

The Expedition

I arrived in New Guinea as a member of the Harvard-Peabody Expedition, which had been organized by Robert Gardner. Gardner is a filmmaker and anthropologist who was head of the Film Study Center in the basement of the Peabody Museum at Harvard. In 1960 he was approached by the director of the Bureau of Native Affairs of the Government of Netherlands New Guinea and invited to take an anthropological expedition to New Guinea. The group which he brought together covered a wide range of skills: Gardner himself would be cameraman and anthropologist; Peter Matthiessen, the natural historian and novelist would write a journal; Michael Rockefeller and Samuel Putnam would do still photography and sound recording; Eliot Elisofon, the *Life* photographer, would back us up on still photography. Jan Broekhuijse, an anthropologist in the Netherlands New Guinea government, was attached to the expedition to help introduce us to the Dani; and Chris Versteegh, a government botanist, joined us for a week to identify the flora. I was then a graduate student in archaeology at Harvard, planning to study the Bronze Age of Thailand. During the summer

The Expedition (1961). Peter Matthiessen, Robert Gardner, and Karl G. Heider behind the lines at a battle. (Photograph by Jan Broekhuijse)

The Expedition (1961). Michael Rockefeller, Jan Broekhuijse, Eliot Elisofon (foreground), and a bemused Um'ue at the Homuak tent camp.

of 1960 I had worked at the Mayan site of Tikal in Guatemala, and, with Gardner's help, had made a film about archaeology and Tikal. In the fall of 1960 when Gardner suggested that I join the New Guinea expedition to do my dissertation and help out with the filming, I immediately accepted.

Gardner arrived in New Guinea first to scout out a suitable place for the expedition work. Fairly certain that we would go to the Grand Valley of the Balim, we had tried to get as much ethnographic and linguistic material on the Dani as possible. But, as an alternative site, Gardner also wanted to visit the Asmat Coast. As it turned out, of course, the Grand Valley was ideal, with easy access to groups which were under neither missionary nor government influence. In February 1961 Gardner met with Broekhuijse in the Grand Valley, and they walked in toward the territory called "Gutelu" (see p. x for pronunciations) after the most important man in that area. They walked in from a mission station on the Balim River and camped the first night on a high ridge. The next day they went on across the no-man's-land which we would all soon get to know. They were not at all certain about their reception on the other side. Gutelu's people had summarily run off outsiders—missionaries and even Broekhuijse—before. In fact, on the far side of a swamp, Gardner and Broekhuijse were suddenly faced by a large army of men armed with spears and bows and arrows. It must have looked a good deal more threatening than it actually was, but neither side knew just what to expect from the other.

Broekhuijse asked to speak with the *gain,* or *ab goktek* ("Big Man"). Much later, people told me with some glee how carefully they had acted that day. They pushed forward a man whose named happened to be Gok ("Big") but who was not really a Big Man, and let him chat with the *tuans* while the real leaders sat to the side. (The Dani used *tuan* for anyone who wore clothes.) It turned out that Gardner had walked into just the right sector of the Gutelu Alliance at just the right time. These people, of the Wiligiman–Walalua Confederation, had been feeling uncomfortable in the Alliance, and were beginning to develop their own independent power; so they were ready to welcome anyone who might be turned to their advantage in their maneuverings against Gutelu. But that day things hung in the air for a time until Um'ue, the quickest of the younger leaders, sized up the situation and stepped forward. He invited them to come live near him. This instant grasp at opportunity was typical of Um'ue. I later came to know him better than I did any other Dani, as a friend and informant, and learned to appreciate and admire his skill. He had seen how useful it could be to have a resident expedition in his midst. For the most part, he was right. It was a long and mutually profitable association.

However, the expedition also led to a chain of misfortunes that none of us could have predicted at the time. Our presence, especially with our movie cameras, focused attention on that area; thus, the Dutch felt compelled eventually to set up a police post there to guarantee pacification. The police post was then the origin of much trouble for the Dani because some factions of Dani became involved on the side of the police—a situation that eventually contributed to renewed warfare in which many Dani were killed and others imprisoned by the Indonesians. Of course it is quite possible that a police post would have been set up in the Dugum Neighborhood even without the expedition. It was certainly a logical place for it. In any case, there were costs as well as benefits from our association with Um'ue.

Even after inviting us to live in his neighborhood, Um'ue moved cautiously. At first we spent more time with two men who more nearly fit the picture of the classic ethnographer's informant, since they were both outsiders to some extent. They hung around our camp, getting to know us and reporting to the community on our strange ways. We were by no means the first outsiders whom these Dani had ever seen, but we were the first who had lived in their midst.

In fact, Um'ue had even taken the precaution of changing his name to Wali, and we knew him as that for the first five months. Then, when Gardner and the rest left, he resumed the name of Um'ue. For the first few days after that I was quite bewildered. People talked about an "Um'ue" who was clearly an important man, but I knew no one by that name. Finally, when I figured it out, I confronted him with this semantic treachery. He explained with a grin: When we first came he had taken a chance in welcoming us, but just in case there should be trouble with the government, it would be blamed on someone named Wali.

Um'ue, who emerged as a major leader during the 1960s, is crossing a flooded ditch on a submerged log. During raids or battles a knowledge of such crossings can give the local people a great advantage over enemy warriors.

On that first visit Gardner and Broekhuijse stayed long enough to get acquainted with the area and to choose a campsite in Homuak, a magnificent grove of araucaria trees where a clear stream issued from the foot of a hill called "Dugum." There, midway between three Dani settlements, we could set up our tents. Our camp was close to people but camouflaged from our cameras, and we avoided the disruption that a dozen people would have caused in a Dani compound.

Rockefeller and I arrived in New Guinea at the end of March 1961. We spent a few days in the administrative center of Hollandia on the coast paying official visits, buying food, and getting our equipment ready for the flight to the Grand Valley. I have now made that flight dozens of times, but it never seems routine. One takes off from the huge airport at Sentani, General MacArthur's command post in World War II, and flies south over the seemingly uninhabited jungle. After half an hour or so the mountains begin to loom ahead. The goal, the Grand Valley of the Balim, is only 1600 meters (5,200 feet) high, but the mountains form a barrier up to 3200 meters (10,000 feet), and the planes must use one of the few narrow passes to get through them. There is always a moment of uncertainty as the pilot searches for an open gap. Weather is unpredictable, and of course there are no weather stations along the front range. That first day, we did not have to turn back. We found a pass clear of clouds and flew through the high broken mountains for a while. On the slopes we could occasionally see a clearing with a thatched house and a garden.

But then, breaking through the mountain wall, we flew out over the broad expanse of the Grand Valley. In 1944 when a U.S. Army plane crashed here, the Grand Valley had been called Shangri-la. Both names are fitting— the valley is magnificent and unexpected. About 45 kilometers (28 miles) long and in places up to 15 kilometers (9 miles) wide, it is a very green, great flat basin with the Balim River meandering down its length. But the most striking change was the signs of humans. For the first 45 minutes of the flight from the coast we saw virtually no hint of humans in the landscape. Here, they were all around. The valley floor has been pretty well forested off in most places, and from the air it seems almost like a park. Everywhere one sees settlements, the clusters of dome-shaped houses and long houses in their clearly defined compounds and clusters of compounds. Around them are the sweet potato gardens and their vast labyrinthine ditchworks. One has suddenly left the trackless wilderness and here, in the very center of New Guinea, comes on a place where culture and cultivation have domesticated an entire landscape. If it has not rained for a while, everywhere across the valley are pillars of smoke, where people are burning off their garden trash. And even in 1961, now and then one could see the sunlight reflecting from the tin roof of a prefabricated missionary house.

Wamena and its airstrip were laid out on land which had been deserted because of a war. The landing strip was built across old garden beds and the patterns of filled-in ditches striped the runway with alternating dark and light grass.

We were met by the entire community of Dutch missionaries and civil servants, curious to see what this expedition was up to. We paid our calls and listened to stories of the Dani which mainly emphasized their strangeness or bloodthirstiness. We got lots of help and some misinformation. My favorite story from that day came from a government official who insisted that the Dani language had no grammatical structure at all, and therefore no European could ever really learn it. I tried to convince him that this was impossible. I should have tried to find out why he said such a thing. (Lost opportunities always hurt. I realized only later that the little community of colonial expatriates at Wamena would have been well worth studying or at least recording. Instead I treated each of my visits there as a relief and vacation from research and never took notes.)

The next day Jan Broekhuijse took us on a little excursion down the river to the compound of Abududi's father. Abududi was the Dani policeman who would be working with us, and Broekhuijse had spent a couple of months before our arrival doing ethnographic work in the compound. Now for the first time we would get a glimpse of real Dani life. Broekhuijse had arranged for the people to cook a pig for us. After a short boat trip we pulled up at the bank where several men were waiting to greet us.

The first man reached out his right hand, and said "Hello." This was too much. I was shaken. To come this far, and be greeted in English this way was a letdown. It turned out not so badly. Dani men often touch on greeting, and it can be a right-hand-to-right-hand handshake. It can also be any other convenient hand-to-arm or even hand-to-body grasp. And he had not said "Hello." It was *halao,* short for *hal-loak-nak,* a standard friendly Dani greeting. (The literal meaning is "let me eat your feces," but no one takes it literally.)

Soon, though, we finished our business at Wamena, moved all our baggage across the valley and set up the tent camp at Homuak. This was to be my home for a year.

For the next five months we all lived in the araucaria grove. During the days we wandered around, each of us on our own tasks. We were out visiting the Dani in their compounds and fields, or we stayed at home to interview the Dani who came to visit us. Since our camp straddled a major thoroughfare, we had plenty of visitors. If something important like a funeral, dance, or battle occurred, we would usually all show up with notebooks and cameras.

The Dani were remarkably tolerant, or perhaps the word really is indifferent. It suited everyone for us to be there but invisible in the background. If nothing of importance was going on, we were mildly entertaining. If something important began, we were quite ignored.

Studying the Women

A major gap in all my Dani work is in the coverage of women. I saw women constantly, observed their activities extensively, and came to know

Mother and child. She wears the married woman's skirt, made of some 30 meters of braided cord. Women usually wear a carrying net on their backs at all times.

some quite well. Especially after I moved into Wubakainma, I was a constant casual part of life in those households. I realized the extent of my acceptance one day when I was in a courtyard alone with a woman. I was waiting for someone, and she was working on a net (see p. 61). Dani women are very modest about their backs. But this one took off her nets to sun her back, and suddenly I realized that I was looking at a Dani woman's bare back for the first time since I had come to the Grand Valley. I was never "initiated into the tribe" or anything like that, but this moment symbolized a sort of acceptance in a quiet Dani manner.

But I was never able to have real discussions with women or to use them as informants. Men, yes; boys, usually; girls, often; but women, almost never. I am still not sure just why. Whenever I tried to ask a woman a question, she would usually just giggle, shake her head, and say she did not know. I suppose that I gave up too easily. In the last few years anthropologists have been made aware of just how important it is to get the women's side of the culture. We—male as well as female anthropologists—have traditionally concentrated on the men, who were the more obvious focus of power and excitement. Now we are coming to recognize not only that women should be studied because they make up half of every population, but also that usually even the "masculine" activities cannot be satisfactorily understood without attending to the women's side. (Of course, this is one of the many lessons which Margaret Mead was trying to teach us decades ago.)

Someday an anthropologist—probably a woman—will examine the women's side of Dani culture. I do not really think that it will drastically change much of what I say here, but it will expand our picture of the Dani significantly.

Coping with the Language

The language problem was always there. None of the local Dani knew any other language. But Abududi, the young man from the lower Grand Valley, who had become a policeman and who worked with Broekhuijse, was our main link. So from the beginning we had some access to Dani: from one of us to Broekhuijse (like most Dutchmen in New Guinea, Jan spoke good English); then in Pasar Malayu (market Malay) to Abududi; and then in Dani to the local people. (People in the eastern half of New Guinea use pidgin English or Neomelanesian, which is an English-based creole; here there was no pidgin, only the basic Indonesian/Malay.) But at best this train of interpreters was a time-consuming process, and so we all learned some Dani. I spent much of these first months seriously working on it, but was handicapped at first by lack of a written grammar. Only months later, when I got a grammar for the lower Grand Valley dialect from Father Piet van der Stap, a linguist working at Wamena, did I realize how much I was missing. Dani verbs are extremely complex. Van der Stap once estimated that with infixes, prefixes, and the like, each Dani verb could have 1680 different forms.

Somehow the Dutch and the Dani had conspired to develop a simplified form of Dani. The verbs were stripped down to one form, the present imperative. Unfortunately, that represented rather accurately the Dutch relations with the Dani, and it was that form which the Dani taught me. Later, with van de Stap's grammar in hand, I worked on real Dani, but despite my pleas, many people would speak with me only in "Police Talk" (as they referred to that language). The Dani are certainly not linguistic chauvinists like, say, Parisians. They were not offended by mistakes; rather, as I learned the simplified grammar or inappropriate words, they would learn them also to accommodate me. I often wondered how the Dani felt about our use of that mangled version of their language. I imagine that they considered us just not very intelligent and not worth the trouble to teach. But Um'ue and some others did understand my wishes and were willing to help me constantly with the language. I always used Dani in speaking, and as I learned real Dani, I became fairly comfortable in conversation. But I never achieved complete fluency. I have tremendous respect for anthropologists who do. Klaus-Friedrich Koch, who studied the Dani-speaking Jalé people just to the northeast of the Grand Valley, got much closer than I. He writes:

> I considered it an attractive challenge to master the transformational rules, but my more sustained intellectual enjoyment came from a gradual comprehension of the metaphorical properties of Jalé speech. The richness of poetic images and the fantastic symbolism of semantic analogies never failed to rouse my admiration. . . . But even in the end I did not understand every talk I heard. Nevertheless I acquired a considerable, if studied, ability to metaphorize my public speech (1974:18).

I wish that I could have written that.

I had a nightmare about the Dani language one night after I had been working on it for several months. I had just translated some songs, and had a real feeling of accomplishment, but I realized that I had reached a sort of plateau in my progress. That night I dreamt: *The Dani actually have four languages, one for each season, and they gradually shift, day to day, from one language to the next.*

Dani children are now learning to read and speak Indonesian in school. Future anthropologists will have to know Indonesian before they get to Dani. In some ways this may make Dani less accessible. But it will also make them bilingual and bicultural with all that implies for perspective, and I think that it will make a tremendous difference in the real accessibility of their culture.

Explaining Ourselves to the Dani

One of the major difficulties underlying fieldwork with the Grand Valley Dani was the fact that they themselves had no touch of the ethnographer in them. They had little contact with other peoples. They were just not curious about other ways of life, and were not practiced in thinking about their own life in that perspective.

Even Um'ue never fully understood what I was doing. He showed tremendous patience in answering my questions, but it was because he was willing to do something which was obviously very important to me. Even he had his limits, though. I had been trying to work out the way in which the Dani conceptualized the sun and the moon, and had gotten somewhat different answers from different people. In cases like that I would often repeat a question to an informant weeks or months later to see if at least he was consistent. So it was that I asked Um'ue for the second or perhaps even third time, "Where does the sun spend the night?" Exasperated, he countered, "In America, don't you have the same sun?" Yes, I had to admit. "Then why do you ask me such questions?" I had always said that I wanted to learn how the Dani do things, and people accepted that at face value since obviously I did not know how to make Dani houses, plant Dani sweet potatoes, or even speak like a Dani. But they did not see that what they knew about the sun was also part of the way that Dani do things and not an essential part of the sun.

They had very little curiosity about us, our homes, our possessions. There were a few standard questions: Where are you from? *Ametiga.* What are your parents called? *Futidisi* (Fritz) and *Egutisi* (Grace). What about your wives and pigs? When I tried to explain that I had neither wife nor pig, they dropped the matter. I suppose that they assumed I must have wives and pigs, but for some reason did not want to talk about them. Perhaps I had gotten into some trouble in Ametiga and had fled. The Dani, being very considerate, would respect my silence. One day, though, a very satisfactory and self-explanatory photograph arrived and I pinned it on my wall: it was of my mother, roasting a dead bird (barbecueing a chicken actually).

We made little effort to explain our material culture to the Dani. At first we never showed them photographs or films of themselves, nor did we explain what cameras could do. We did not want to make them camera conscious, and we did not want to take a chance that they would think the cameras somehow magically threatening. In later years the children, especially, did become terrible muggers whenever a camera appeared. But I think that we worried needlessly about the Dani fears. In 1970 I took copies of our photographic ethnography, *Gardens of War* (Gardner and Heider 1969), to the Grand Valley. Dani loved to leaf through it. They recognized without any misgivings pictures of themselves, their friends, and even people who had since died or had been killed.

There were some potential complications with medicine. For example, I, like most outsiders, gave penicillin shots, which were to treat yaws or framboesia (a tropical skin ulcer.) It is a sure cure. One missionary told me that when he gave penicillin shots, he had the patient pray with him to Jesus. Then, when the yaws were cured, he would point out that the Dani owed the cure to Jesus. In a similar example of using medicine as a tool of conversion, a missionary physician refused to treat fingers which had festered after being chopped off (for a discussion of Dani finger mutilation, see p. 133). I made no claims for the *wusa,* or sacredness of my medicines, and no Dani misunderstood it. I treated people whenever they asked (and I thought I could help), but the Dani were extremely healthy, and I had little to do.

I did have some little wind-up, spark-spitting toys which children loved to use to scare newcomers (especially traders from the Jalémo, who have a reputation for extreme gullibility in the Grand Valley). But I tried to give rational explanations for objects, even when I did not fully understand them myself. I think that I was successful, although once Um'ue came to my house to ask about my radio:

> "Can you talk into the radio and find lost pigs?" (Dani sometimes use divination for that purpose.)
> "No," I said, "why do you ask?"
> "Well, I didn't think so myself, but some people from over there say that radios can do that, so I thought I would ask just in case."

The Months Alone

At the end of August 1961 the expedition disbanded and everyone went his own way. Robert Gardner returned to his studio at Harvard where he spent the next 18 months editing the footage for a film which he would call *Dead Birds*. Peter Matthiessen went home via the Great Barrier Reef to write a book about the Dani called *Under the Mountain Wall*. Samuel Putnam returned to his classes at Harvard Medical School; Jan Broekhuijse resumed his government post and eventually wrote his dissertation for Utrecht University on the Dani. Michael Rockefeller traveled through the Asmat Coast to collect the magnificent wood-carvings for the Museum of Primitive Art, and there he died in November 1961. The circumstances of his death were never conclusively established. The various theories include drowning, sharks, or cannibals. So it is perhaps sadly inevitable that his disappearance has been the subject of an astonishing number of sensational reports in print and television. He left two real monuments: first, the great collection of Asmat art, most of it fragile wood pieces which would have long since rotted away in the jungles if he had not felt the mission to preserve them; and second, his fine photographs both of the Asmat (in Gerbrands 1967) and of the Dani (in Gardener and Heider 1969).

I consolidated the tent camp at Homuak, sharing it with Jusup Kakiay, an elderly South Moluccan man who had once been cook and bird preparer for S. Dillon Ripley, the ornithologist at Yale. Jusup cooked for the expedition and then, when the others left, spent a couple of months collecting and preparing birds from the Grand Valley for Ripley, and cooking for me on the side. I suppose that during those months I tasted more species of birds than in all the years before or since.

Having the expedition there had many advantages. With all of us out exploring the countryside constantly, we found out much that one person would have missed. And, of course, it was always good to be able to talk about things and puzzle over them in such congenial company. We all enjoyed each other and listened with some smugness to stories of a previous New Guinea expedition where the members were reduced to sending each other notes in order to avoid having to talk.

When everyone had gone, and I settled into the camp alone, I was suddenly overcome with loneliness. Shortly thereafter I spent the day at a funeral, and in the late afternoon, as things quieted down, returned to my tent to eat and type up my notes while events were still fresh. It was then that I particularly missed the opportunity to review the day with the others. On a whim I decided to go back to the funeral compound—it was Um'ue's, where I felt most at home—and stayed the night in the men's house. We had followed several funerals quite carefully by then, and I was confident that I knew the general course of that particular Dani ceremony at least. I was not at all prepared for the general stir in the compound just before dawn. Some of the young men were preparing for another ritual task. I got up and followed them out of the compound to a nearby hilltop where they made a circle of plucked grass, ate some of the funeral pork, and generally directed the ghost of the newly dead person toward the enemy frontier. I sat on the hilltop, soaked in the night dew, taking notes. With one part of my mind I was wrapped in the casual private beauty of the ritual; with the rest I was furious at myself for having missed so much by yielding to the luxury of the expedition camp so many nights.

I was continually stumbling across things like that. I am quite sure that it was not the Dani's intention to hide things from me. But they just did not bother to tell me about them. They liked me, but they were not much concerned about anthropology. I could never ask anyone, "Tell me all about what happens at a funeral." I had to attend myself, take notes, and later ask for explanations point by point. Then people would be quite forthcoming.

Even after the chastening night of discovery at the funeral, I used various ways to escape. I opened a charge account at Swain's Bookstore on Castelreigh Street in Sydney and ordered huge batches of novels. I would sometimes read for a day and a night, ignoring Dani completely. I always listened to the radio—the news, the features, everything—even dramatic play-by-play accounts of exotic Australian games which I still have never actually seen. Every couple of weeks I would make the walk alone across the Grand Valley to Wamena to pick up mail and supplies. The trip would take between two hours and four hours, depending on how muddy the paths and pole bridges were and how long I would have to wait at the Balim River for a raft to ferry me across. In Wamena I usually visited the Dutch Franciscan missionaries, well-educated men who liked to drink wine, play chess, argue about politics or the Dani, and especially discuss the two Johns, my president and their pope. My most important contact during this time was Denise O'Brien, a graduate student from Yale, who was doing fieldwork among the Western Dani of the Konda Valley, some 50 kilometers away. There was someone who was deeply concerned with the same sorts of great and small discoveries about Dani culture. We wrote back and forth at every opportunity. Since Grand Valley Dani and Western Dani are so closely related, this constant comparison gave each of us valuable perspectives.

After the others left, and Jusup Kakiay left, I stayed on in the old tent camp. The great advantage of that location was that many people had easy access to me, but I missed constant intimate contact with one compound. Um'ue had been urging me to move nearer to his compound at Wubakainma, just a few minutes' walk from the tent camp. Finally, after a year in the tents

I built a house in Wubakainma and spent my second year there in constant range of all the sights, sounds, and smells that mark the pace of Dani domestic life.

In October 1962, at the end of 18 months, I took a six-month break from the Dani. I returned to Harvard to collect my thoughts, work over my field notes, discuss the progress of my dissertation, and help Gardner in the final stages of editing his film *Dead Birds.*

By this time, jurisdiction over the territory was slowly and diplomatically being transferred from the Netherlands to Indonesia, via a unique interim government, the United Nations Temporary Executive Authority. This transition is a fascinating chapter in international affairs, but the Dani were almost totally unaware of what was going on.

When I returned to Wubakainma in March 1962, it was as if I had never been away. The Dani greeted me casually, with their usual warmth but without surprise. I had left my belongings in my house, protected only by the people's goodwill and a knotted grass taboo sign on the door. Six months later the door was ajar, and grass had grown up knee high from the floor, but nothing was gone. This second visit lasted nine months, and during that time I worked on my dissertation, shot footage for what would become the two films, *Dani Sweet Potatoes* and *Dani Houses,* and I waited for the Pig Feast.

The major climactic Dani ceremony, the great Pig Feast, takes place every five or six years. It had been promised ever since we arrived. In April 1961 the Dani said that it was six months away. Two years later it was still six months away. The problem was that the Dani do not break time up into units like months. While they were willing to go along with our ideas and count off "new moons" on their fingers, they were not about to schedule their lives in our terms. By September 1963 there were definite signs of the Pig Feast, but by November it was still not in sight. I was due back at Harvard for the spring semester, and so, in early December 1963 I left New Guinea, after some 26 months there. The Pig Feast started a few weeks later (see p. 138).

Returning Later

During the next few years I finished my dissertation, which was a very general ethnography of the Dani, began teaching at Brown University, and prepared to return to the Dani, this time to work in collaboration with Eleanor Rosch, an experimental cognitive psychologist. In 1968 we spent seven weeks with the Dani and in 1970 seven months. This fieldwork was very different from what I did during my first two visits. We lived at a Catholic mission station about an hour's walk from my old neighborhood and close by the huge settlement of Jibiga, where Gutelu lived. In addition to the mission, there was a school, a first aid station, an Indonesian army post and police post, and a small landing field.

In 1966 there had been a short and very bloody war which split the old Gutelu Alliance in two. All my old friends were now joined with some of their former enemies to the South in a new Alliance, lead by Um'ue and a southerner, Obagatok. However, despite the ferocity of the fighting only two years earlier, there was surprisingly little bitterness. Um'ue and his people often came to Jibiga along the government road to do business with officials, or to visit me; in fact, some of their children attended school at Jibiga. Once while leaders of both sides were visiting me, I inadvertently tripped off a discussion of the 1966 events and then listened in amazement as the men calmly swapped stories of how they had killed each others' families and friends.

Our main research in both 1968 and 1970 was a series of very directed interviews and experiments. Instead of visiting compounds, we spent most of the time at tables working with one Dani after another. Often the schoolteachers would help us by sending one schoolchild after the other from the schoolroom to work with us. This arrangement pleased all concerned.

In 1970, at last, I saw a Pig Feast. This was actually a mixed blessing. It engaged the entire Alliance for the 17 days of the ceremony and long before and afterward. Our experiments were totally disrupted. But it was my first opportunity finally to see this most important of all Dani ceremonies.

The difference between this Pig Feast in June 1970 and the battles and ceremonies which we observed in June 1961 was remarkable. The Dani themselves had not changed much. But now the world had joined in. The Pig Feast was a media event. A joint Japanese-Indonesian television crew flew in to cover it; missionaries from elsewhere in New Guinea and even tourists came to watch. Father Jules Camps' mission station took on the aspect of a hotel, and his facilities were stretched to bursting. But the Pig Feast, like other Dani ceremonies, was not designed by a tourist bureau for photographic appeal, and most of the visitors went away disappointed. At any rate, the Dani of the Grand Valley had joined the stream of world culture.

Ethical Problems

It is not possible to do this sort of fieldwork without being taken by surprise by many sorts of ethical problems. We can live our lives as normally responsible, reasonably honest persons in our own society and not ever be surprised in that way. We have a pretty good idea of the norms and of the consequences of most of our acts, but all this is of little help in the field. Not only is the culture more or less unknown (that is the reason for being there in the first place, of course), but usually there is little precedent for the particular role of outsider which the anthropologist wishes to play. Most anthropologists study down; that is, we study relatively poor, powerless tribes, subcultures, or minority groups. We suddenly find ourselves transformed from frugal graduate students into fabulously rich and powerful creatures in charge of domestic establishments which include houseboys, cooks, carriers, and the like. All this was true in the classical colonial situation—with one profound difference: The colonials came to exercise power, in the name of their Religion or Order, or of the Road or the Canal. The ethnographer has come to live among the people as the most ignorant of them all, hoping to learn in a few months everything that everyone knows. And so, assuming ignorance and rejecting power, the anthropologist is soon backed into many hopeless quandries.

For example, one day in 1961, a few months after we had arrived and when warfare was going on, a woman from an enemy alliance crossed into the territory where we lived. Our friends had just lost two lives to the enemy spears, and were quite anxious to reestablish some balance by killing one of the enemy. This woman would certainly have been killed had not one of us heard of her arrival, walked over the the village, and spirited her away. This meant only that the killing was postponed, and indeed, within a few days an enemy man was killed. We could not have left the woman to die, yet even as we saved her we could be certain that we were dooming someone else. As it happened, the man was killed near our camp. We heard the noise as we were finishing diner, and ran to investigate. I was the first to arrive, and by then the man was dead, riddled with spear wounds. I have often wondered what I would have done, and what I could have done, if I had arrived a minute earlier, or five minutes, or ten minutes.

Or take a quite different sort of dilemma: During the first year and a half of my stay, the Dani were under the control of the government of Netherlands New Guinea. Sometimes during the Dutch period a government official—usually a policeman—would use his power against the Dani to steal, brutalize, or rape. In a couple of instances Dani men came to me and explained the situation. I sent notes to the higher official and the situation was corrected, or at least the culprit was recalled. The Dutch were not very pleased with my interference, but they respected it and always took action. Then, in 1963, power over the Dani was transferred to Sukarno's Indonesia, and circumstances at that time were not such that American interference was welcomed at all. Police were under less control, and Dani complaints to me increased, but the Dani were unable to understand why I now refused to intervene. Once, when things got very bad, I did intervene against my better judgment. And I did make the situation worse.

I should add that these sorts of incidents were caused by low-level police and military, people who were most unhappy to find themselves posted to the uncivilized West Irian. Officials at higher levels were very favorably disposed to anthropology, and they asked for my advice. But my recommendations were mainly negative: It would not be feasible to ship all Dani children to schools on the coast, or to move all Dani into villages along a single road going up the middle of the Grand Valley, or to move the pig sties far away from the houses for sanitary purposes (pig thefts would have skyrocketed.)

There were constant smaller things: I paid the Dani with shells, steel axes, and finally money for help, firewood, food, information, and stone axes and other museum artifacts, all of which were worth much more to me than I paid for them. But I gave up trying to work out a fair rate of exchange—my one reservation was that I bought only stone axes or adzes for metal tools.

Although I have no medical training, I did have an extensive medical kit, and I dispensed antiobiotics and penicillin in a way that I would never be permitted to do in the United States. For years I was proud of my role (along with missionaries) in wiping out yaws, but recently I have heard that syphilis is entering the Grand Valley. I now wonder if the yaws might have given some immunity to syphilis. But with that immunity now gone, the Dani are vulnerable to the worse disease.

The most complex ethical dilemma concerned the Harvard-Peabody Expedition and Dani warfare. We were accused of starting wars so that we could film the Dani in battle. This report got into the press, and although I tried to deal with it in print (1970:16), even now when I visit a new campus to talk about the Dani, someone always asks if it is true we paid for wars or encouraged them. The answer is definitely and unequivocably no. We arrived in the midst of a war and observed some eight battles, but we did not request or pay for them. Even here the answer is too simple. We were obviously interested in battles. We asked about them, and we did not discourage them or disapprove of them. We were the only outsiders of the Grand Valley who were not trying to change the Dani, and whose mandate was to watch their rituals and their conflict in an attempt to understand, not to censure. It was difficult for the Dani to understand what we were doing and why we were so different from the other *tuans.* It was even more difficult for the other *tuans,* the missionary and government people. They felt that despite what we said, our very presence at battles or at rituals gave a kind of implicit approval to these events. Slowly we all came to understand and appreciate each other's goals and problems, and I developed tremendous respect for many of them. But to the end, we stepped on each other's toes.

These were some of the ethical problems which I faced. Most anthropologists could tell stories about similar ones. There are no easy answers. But the problems cannot be brushed away as figments of fashionable liberal guilt. One of the many advances in the anthropology of the last decade is that we are trying to deal with these problems and preparing our students to meet them.

ADVENTURE TWO: THE HOMEWORK

I first went to the Dani to study stone axes. I had been trained in archaeology, where my concern was with the classification and interpretation of artifacts. The Dani were using stone tools similar to those of the ancient Mayans of Guatemala, where I had dug. With Mayan tools one soon comes to a dead end because the people are no longer around. The Dani offered an excellent opportunity to look at stone tools in use and to talk with their users—an approach now called ethno-archaeology. So, during my first few months in New Guinea I worked on Dani artifacts, counting, measuring, naming, photographing their use, and so forth. For a while I thought of focusing the entire study on the men's house, analyzing it in detail and working out its relations with all other aspects of Dani culture. I did write an article and much of my first monograph on those concerns (Heider 1967a, 1967b, and 1970). But gradually my interests shifted from the stone adze to the person holding it, from the material aspects of culture to the mental phenomena which make up culture.

Changing Views

I started trying to understand the Dani in 1961, and 16 years later I was still working on it. During that time I had to change my mind about a number of things. Perhaps this was because I was fortunate enough to have been able to visit New Guinea four times over a period of nine years. This meant that between trips I could think out my data and devise new questions for the next trip. Also, over the nine years I was able to see a little of the process of change in Dani society, certainly more than I could have if I had had to depend on a one-year glimpse, augmented only by Dani recollections of how things had happened. Also I was most fortunate in my colleagues, those others who were working with the Dani at the same time that I was and whose different perspectives helped me tremendously.

The story of the various mistakes and false leads which I started out on is revealing both of the Dani culture and of the preconceptions which even anthropologists bring from their own cultures.

First Revision: The Disaster of Pacification   During the first five months of fieldwork I observed many battles, funerals, and so forth which were part of the war between our friends of the Gutelu Alliance and their enemies, the Widaia. Unfortunately, because at that time I had only the beginning of a command of the language and I was conscientiously working on my artifact study, I was not able to get as much immediate information about warfare as I might have. But even so, it became clear how deeply embedded Dani war was in the culture. Again and again I came across evidence of the central role of war in Dani life.

During those months, whenever I made the trek to Wamena, I discussed this with the Dutch officials. Their task was to pacify the entire valley. They had been successful in the southern valley around Wamena, but elsewhere their efforts had been sporadic and their results spotty. Two years earlier they had sent an armed patrol into the Gutelu region to stop the fighting. They shot and killed one man, and for a few months there were no battles. But the Grand Valley is huge, patrols were few, and when the Dutch did not reappear, the Dani resumed warfare. Now the Dutch would have to take stronger steps. In 1961 the confrontation between the Netherlands and Indonesia over the fate of West New Guinea was beginning to heat up, and the United Nations debate was focusing world attention on the territory. The

Dutch could not afford to have tribal wars going on under their administration, especially one which would be publicized by a film from the Harvard Expedition.

I agreed with the Dutch that they had no political choice but to go in and end Dani warfare. However, I spent a lot of time trying to make them understand the holistic concept of culture and see that one could not expect to remove a major institution like war without undermining all of Dani culture. Particularly if one ended war as an outlet for violence and aggression, one would have to expect it to reemerge elsewhere. So the government must be prepared for a great upsurge in suicide, homicide, and other forms of within-group violence.

In September 1961 the Dutch did end the warfare in the Gutelu area. During the months that followed, I waited for the violence. It did not come. I had been wrong. This experience made me rethink a number of things. First, the holistic model cannot be taken too literally. In a cultural system parts are interrelated in various ways, more or less internally. Warfare touched many parts of Dani life but was not essential to many. Previously, I tried to explain this by pointing to Dani pragmatism (1970:123–134): When the Dutch force made war impossible (or too costly), the Dani accommodated their culture to this new fact. Now I am willing to go even further and to suggest that warfare was in many respects not consistent, or even strikingly inconsistent, with the basic pattern of Dani culture, and therefore relatively easily ended (see p. 119).

Second Revision: Ecological Effects of War   For the first few years I was quite misled about Dani warfare because I had seen only one aspect of it, the ritual phase, which had been underway in 1961. I never had much success in getting Dani to talk at length about the past. As a result, I understood only the fairly static, 10-year-long pace of the ritual phase, which was explained by the Dani as necessary to placate their ghosts. While I was writing up my materials on the Dani in the mid-1960s, several anthropologists at Columbia and the University of Michigan were looking at tribal warfare in eastern New Guinea in primarily ecological terms (see especially Vayda and Rappaport 1968). My data seemed to be a strong counterargument: Dani warfare had little or no effect on ecological variables like population density. In any case, I reacted against the primacy of a single (materialistic) explanation, for having seen warfare taking place, I was concerned with the various different sorts of causes and effects which embedded warfare in Dani life. Fortunately, in 1968, before I could publish all this, I returned to the Dani and immediately learned the details about a major conflict which had wracked the old Gutelu Alliance. Many missionaries told me their versions, and armed with these basic details, I was able to get much more information from the Dani who had participated. Then I was able to follow it up by working out historical accounts of similar events which I had heard vaguely about before but had never really understood.

This secular phase of war, which punctuates the ritual phase and rearranges alliances every 10 years or so, is very different from the ritual phase, and it does have considerable material effect on the Dani—populations shift, goods are destroyed, and so forth. Had I not returned for a third visit to the Dani in 1968, I would probably still now be propagating a badly incomplete version of Dani conflict.

Third Revision: The Pattern of Culture   The third major revision was not a matter of finding new information, but rather of slowly moving from descriptions of events (like funerals) or analyses of specific cognitive realms (like kinship terms) to a broader level where I could make generalizations about the patterns of Dani culture. We often think at this higher level in ordinary life. We ask and answer questions like: "What do you think of the people here in South Carolina (or Kansas or California)?" "What are they like in France (or Mexico)?" But in anthropology we are so concerned with establishing and analyzing the basic facts of a culture that we rarely move to the higher level. Also, we seldom have the opportunity for enough fieldwork or enough writing time to get that far. I have been very lucky in this respect, for I was given both opportunity and time.

As I first tried to work out the data, there were a few facts which seemed more and more unexplainable. Finally, they began to make sense as part of a larger pattern of Dani culture. The most startling of these apparent anomalies is the Dani postpartum sexual abstinence—a five-year period after the birth of the child when the parents do not have sexual intercourse with each other. This practice seemed very surprising to everyone I described it to, but in my first ethnography I spent only one page on it (1970:74–75). However, it would not rest, so I followed it out, returning two more times for deeper fieldwork. Finally, I think that now we can understand the low Dani interest in sexuality as part of a pattern of low psychic energy (although the Dani themselves are normally intelligent, healthy, and have plenty of physical energy). This pattern of Dani culture will be referred to throughout the book (also see Heider ms.).

Dead Birds in Retrospect   Finally, in talking about changing understandings about the Dani, I should mention the film *Dead Birds.* This film has been responsible for making the Dani one of the better-known tribal cultures to introductory anthropology classes. But the footage was shot in 1961, and editing finished in 1963. How, then, does the film stand up today in the face of all these new facts and ideas about the Dani? Amazingly well, I think, thanks mainly to Robert Gardner's great skill as both filmmaker and anthropologist. In many respects he was far ahead of me in understanding the Dani. When he brought the first version of *Dead Birds* back to New Guinea in a brief visit in 1962, I came out of the Grand Valley, and we had a gala screening at the Governor's Palace in Hollandia. I was dubious then about his emphasis on the man-as-bird symbolism, which is one major structural motif of the film. When I returned to the Grand Valley and dug into the matter, it turned out that he had seen a theme that was not only good cinema, but true for the Dani as well.

When I returned to Harvard briefly in the winter of 1962–1963, I worked over the narration of the film, but still there are a few minor slips that got by.

I would now change the line "sharpening bone with stone" to the less euphonious but more accurate "sharpening pig tusk with flint."

The warfare shown in *Dead Birds* is only the ritual phase of war, of course. We had no opportunity to film the secular phase and indeed, I had only the foggiest notion that it ever existed. The film would have given a fuller picture of Dani warfare if it had at least mentioned this secular phase in the narration. But I had not yet begun to understand that part of warfare when we were making the film. It obviously is better to make such films at the end, rather than the beginning, of extended fieldwork.

In retrospect, through, the main fault of the film is that it does not reflect very well the Dani pattern of low psychic energy. However, in 1961 we were not thinking in those terms. We came from a culture of high psychic energy, a culture which, in countless ways celebrates peak experiences. We came looking for the important events of Dani life and focused on those rare peak moments which we did find. Actually, even in a battle or a funeral most of the participants are relaxed and calm most of the time. But in editing the film, the periods of calm were slighted and the peak moments spliced together to create an effect of sustained high-intensity action.

In fact, it is remarkable that Gardner did capture much of this Dani casualness in the film. But since most audiences are from the same high-energy culture as we, they tend to see and to remember the peak moments.

Two years after *Dead Birds* was filmed, I shot footage for two short films on Dani technology (Heider 1974a, 1974b). These films capture the casual pace of Dani life much better, but this success is due more to the everyday subject matter than to my own insights at that time.

I certainly do not intend this point to be a debunking of *Dead Birds.* It is a film with scientific as well as aesthetic qualities, and as a scientific report it would be surprising if it had not been superseded in part at least by the findings from subsequent fieldwork. At any rate, it does reflect the understanding which both Gardner and I had of the Dani in 1962, after my first 18 months of fieldwork.

2 / The Dani

INTRODUCTION TO THE DANI

The Dani are one among many peoples who speak related Papuan, or non-Austronesian, languages and live in the high central ranges of New Guinea. Until the last few decades these Papuans were some of the most isolated people in the world, protected as they were from the coastal populations by swamps and mountains. They grew root crops (mainly sweet potatoes), raised pigs, and used polished stone axes and adzes. They did not make pottery, but otherwise their technology was very much like that of the Neolithic of the Old and New Worlds.

There may be 200,000 Dani living in the central mountains. Like the Western Dani of the Konda or the Jalé of the East, many live scattered along the steep mountain slopes. The Dani of this study live in large settlements on the flat floor of the Grand Valley of the Balim River. In 1961 when I began this study, the Dani of the Gutelu Alliance were not yet under Dutch government control. They did have a few steel tools, but although their technology was still Stone Age, they lived on the brink of change and literally within sight of the airplanes which daily crossed the Grand Valley. In 1970 when I last visited them, the entire Grand Valley was under Indonesian government control, warfare was more or less ended, steel tools outnumbered stone, and police posts, schools, and mission stations were everywhere. In this study I shall deal with the Dani as they were until 1961, and also as they changed during the next decade.

Two Styles of Introduction

There are a couple of ways to get a quick introduction to the Dani. One way is to look at photographs. The photographs in this book will give a pretty good idea of the appearance of the Dani environment, of their bodies, and of the external aspects of their behavior. But much of Dani culture—indeed the most interesting parts, having to do with meanings and ideas—is of course quite inaccessible to the camera. In a few instances photographs would even be misleading. But it is interesting to speculate how far one could get writing an ethnography if one could only look at a few photographs.

25

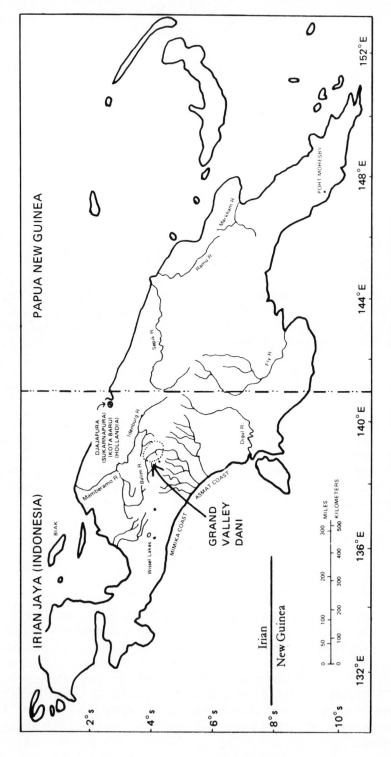

Map 1. Irian (New Guinea). (Heider 1970:298)

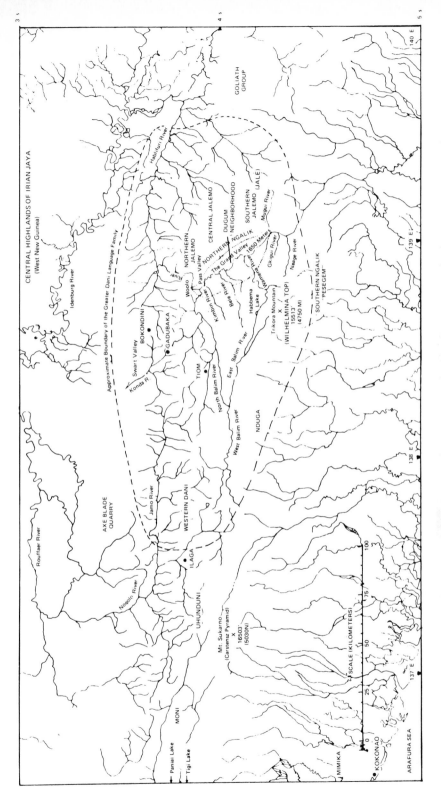

Map 2. *The central highlands of Irian Jaya (West New Guinea). (Heider 1970:299)*

27

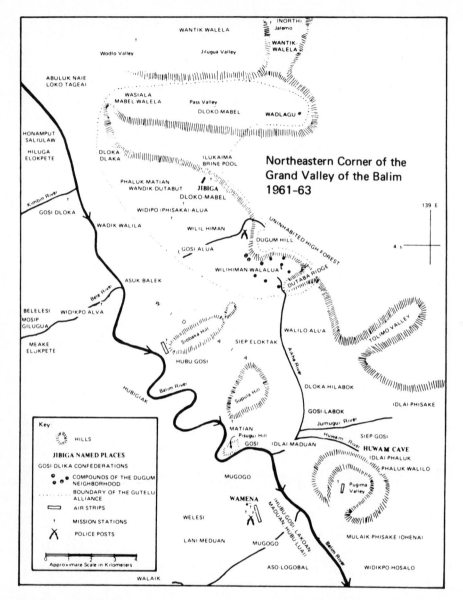

Map 3. Northeastern corner of the Grand Valley of the Balim, 1961–1963.
(Heider 1970:300)

A second sort of introduction is to ask the people themselves. During my fourth trip to the Dani, I did just that as a systematic experiment (described in detail in Heider 1975a). I sat outside a schoolhouse with pencil and notebook, and the children came out to me one by one. I asked 60 schoolchildren the very simple question, "What do people do?" and kept repeating the question until each had given me 50 responses.

It happens that Dani has a verb form, the habitual aspect, which is used for culturally expectable, habitual activity. It might almost be called the ethnographic aspect, since it is so useful for discussing the sorts of things which we try to find out about the normal cultural patterns in a society. So there was a ready-made question: "What do people do?" And the answer was almost always in the same concise form; for example, "They plant sweet potatoes."

I have assumed that the order of the responses reflected in some way the Dani sense of what was salient or important about their own cultures. For

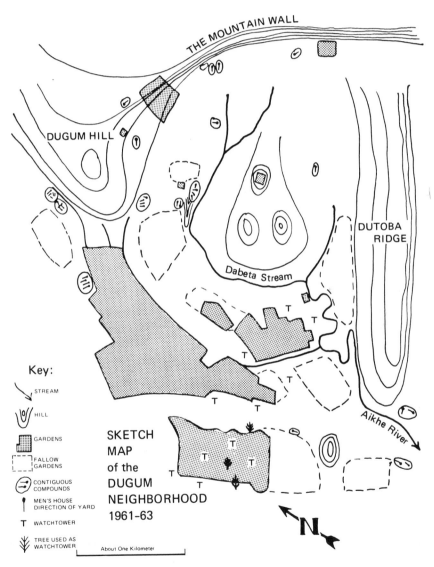

Map 4.   *The Dugum neighborhood, 1961–1963. (Heider 1970:301)*

the purpose of analysis I broke the subjects down into three groups: 20 young girls (about 6 to 10 years old); 20 boys about the same age; and 20 boys about 12 to 18 years old. Table 2.1 shows the pattern of the very first responses, and Table 2.2 shows the first 10 responses for each person.

The picture which the Dani give of their own culture is very different from what captures our attention. The Dani talk about raising food and cooking it, not about war or ceremonies. (At the time I asked these questions, no warfare was going on, but they were in the midst of the great Pig

TABLE 2.1   THE VERY FIRST RESPONSE OF EACH OF 60 DANI TO THE QUESTION "WHAT DO PEOPLE DO," ARRANGED BY MAJOR ACTIVITY REALM AND BY THE THREE SEX AND AGE GROUPS OF 20 PEOPLE EACH

Realm of Activity	Activity	Young	Younger	Older
Gardens	Make gardens	1	2	9
	Harvest a vegetable	1	0	0
	Harvest sweet potato	2	0	0
	Cut a vegetable	1	0	0
	Harvest	1	0	0
	Get greens	0	1	0
	Turn soil	0	6	6
	Plant	0	1	1
Food preparation	Steam food	8	0	1
	Eat	0	2	1
	Wash sweet potato	0	1	0
	Gather firewood	0	1	1
Other		6	6	1

(from Heider 1975a:6)

TABLE 2.2   RESPONSES TO THE QUESTION "WHAT DO PEOPLE DO," ARRANGED BY MAJOR ACTIVITY REALM AND BY SEX AND AGE GROUPS*

Realm of Activity	Young Girls	Younger Boys	Older Boys	Total
Gardening	40	62	74	176
Food preparation	63	35	40	138
Construction	0	10	18	28
Hunting and gathering	10	10	7	27
Pigs	7	6	6	19
Ceremonies	2	4	10	16
Tools	0	1	4	5
Social conflict	3	4	3	10
Other	19	9	6	34
			Grand total	453

*Each group consisted of 20 people. This table calculates only the first 10 (of the total 50) responses of each person. Because of repetitions the grand total falls short of the possible 600.
(from Heider 1975a:8)

Feast.) A particularly striking feature of these lists is the virtual absence of interpersonal behavior.

I have called this an "autoethnography" because it is an automatic sort of questioning technique and also because it gives an autochthonous, or native, view of the culture. So, in this Dani autoethnography, we see industrious farmers who are peaceful to the point of not getting very much involved with each other at all.

Although the rest of the book will talk much more about war and cere-monies and social relations, we shall also discuss the Dani cultural pattern of low psychic energy. The Dani autoethnography certainly does not tell us all that we want to know, but as we shall see, it does touch on this very basic general pattern of Dani life.

The Name "Dani"

These people did not call themselves "Dani." Actually, this is true of most of the peoples of the world: Eskimo, Sioux, Chinese, Dutch, and Indians. None are their own names, and all too often they are derogatory words in a neighboring language. At least *Dani* does not seem to be derogatory. It is not clear where it comes from, but it is widely used in the literature as a conve-nient label for a large number of peoples who inhabit the drainage of the Balim and other rivers in central western New Guinea. These peoples speak different but closely related languages, have different but closely related cultures, and live in many quite independent political units. In this sense, then, there is no single Dani tribe or language or culture.

The term *Grand Valley Dani* refers to a subgroup: the 50,000 or so people (no one has yet tried to count them) who live in the Grand Valley of the Balim River. (At either end of the Grand Valley live a few western and southern Dani.) They all speak the same language, but in the 45-kilometer length of the Grand Valley one finds different dialects—some different sounds, a few dif-ferent words, and some grammatical variation. But basically, we can say that the Grand Valley Dani have a common language and culture. In the early 1960s I worked mainly on one 350-person neighborhood, which I call the "Dugum Neighborhood." It is part of one 1000-person confederation, which the Dani call "Wilihiman–Walalua." The Confederation was then still part of one 5000-person alliance, which we call the "Gutelu Alliance," in the Grand Valley. There are about 10 alliances in the Grand Valley. Out of extreme caution I titled my first ethnography *The Dugum Dani* to indicate that I was speaking about only those 350 people. But most of the important things which I am saying here are valid for the entire Grand Valley, and so, with some trepidation, I am calling this study *Grand Valley Dani*. (If I am seriously challenged, I shall retreat, saying that I only mean "some Grand Valley Dani.")

It may well happen that some day the Dani will develop a sense of their own cultural unity and will need their own term to signify and politicize this consciousness. Now they do speak of *nit akhuni Balim-mede* ("we, the

Balim people") in contrast to *akhuni Jalimo-mede* ("the Jalé people"). Perhaps they, or some leader, will choose the word *akhuni,* "people." Meanwhile, we can use the term *Dani.*

The Dani Language

Until 1954, when missionaries were the first Europeans to trickle into the Grand Valley, most Dani had never met anyone who did not speak their own language. Sometimes on trading trips they had run into people who spoke different dialects. Since missionary settlements began, however, they have heard other languages, and by 1970 a major attempt was being made to teach the children to speak Indonesian. They are certainly aware of the dialect variations within the Grand Valley, and distinguish between their own speech, which is *ane mot* ("straight talk"), and that of the others, who speak *ane goto* ("twisted, or crooked talk"; also "lies"). But on the whole, Dani are not linguistic chauvinists—I have described how tolerant they were of my own mistakes.

Grand Valley Dani language is characterized by verbs which are highly inflected and nouns which are usually not inflected at all (only a few have both singular and plural forms). Van der Stap, in his *Outline of Dani Morphology* (1966), spent 138 pages on verbs but dealt with all other categories in just 14 pages. And practically all of Bromley's 635-page dissertation on Dani grammar is concerned with verbs. I often visited van der Stap in the mission station at Wamena to compare notes on my dialect from midvalley with his on the southern dialect around the station. I would usually find him puzzling over Dani verbs. Once in amazement and admiration, he said that one could almost speak Dani with the verbs alone, for they carried so much information.

A question which we can ask about the Dani language is one which has long fascinated anthropologists: What is the relation between language and culture? This question was raised by Karl Wilhelm von Humboldt, the nineteenth-century German scholar, and it reemerged in American anthropological linguistics as the Sapir–Whorf hypothesis in the 1930s.

Several features of the language do seem consistent with other aspects of the culture:

1. The Dani have one word for "sweet potato," but then have dozens of names for sweet potato varieties. One would expect this of a people whose main food is sweet potato (in contrast with most Americans who rarely eat sweet potato and who confuse the sweet potato and the yam).

When I started out to collect sweet potato names, I soon had about 70, which seemed like a lot for any one person to remember. I tried to work out the system of these words, and it turned out that different people would call the same tuber by different names. Then I looked at names for axe and adze stones and found the same thing: a huge vocabulary inconsistently used. (These experiments are described in Heider ms.)

It is not surprising to find many words used to make minute distinctions in areas of particular cultural concern, but it is surprising to find these words being used inconsistently. After all, if language is to be communication, then people must agree on meanings. I cannot explain this Dani disagreement. Actually, we do not yet have enough comparable data from other cultures to know how unusual this Dani situation is. But it seems to me that it makes sense in the context of a general Dani pattern of casualness and lack of complex intellectualization. It is not known when all these words for sweet potato emerged, but in the light of other Dani behavior it is not surprising that they are not structured into a single elegant system.

2. We find a somewhat similar phenomenon with numbers. Dani have only four number words: *magiat* (one), *pete* (two, or pair), *henaken* (three), and *modok* (many). Years ago, when I read reports of languages in which one could not count to 10, I was skeptical, and thought that they were only credulous travelers' tales. Now it turns out to be quite different.

The point is that the Dani get along very well without quantifying their environment. In other cultures, numbers are useful for tallying masses of identical things like monetary units. But the Dani do not use money. Or numbers can be useful for dealing with masses of similar things if one is willing first to consider them as identical and then tally them. But the Dani do not make that abstraction. If a man has a herd of pigs, it is rarely more than a dozen or two, and he can keep in mind the age, sex, and markings of his individual pigs. At a funeral, the people who were concerned could keep track of what sort of pig was brought by whom and add it to their knowledge of the current state of gifts and debts within the group. I would go to a funeral and sit counting the number of pigs, and in the end I could say, "this was a 24-pig funeral." A Dani would know other, richer things about the funeral, but he would not be interested in such a tally.

Other highland Papuan groups do have more elaborate number systems. The most common one is based on the number 27 or 28 or thereabouts. This base may sound unusual, but that is the number reached if you begin counting on one little finger, go up touching several points along one arm, across the top of the head, down the other arm to the other little finger. The Egaki (or Kapauku), who live to the west of the Dani, are obsessed with quantification and can count into the tens of thousands (see Pospisil 1958, 1963).

The lack of a complex number vocabulary is another bit of evidence for the low concern which the Dani have with intellectualizing their world.

3. Finally, it is difficult to make comparisons with Dani adjectives or adverbs. In English we use comparative and superlative forms frequently, a practice consistent with our concern for competition, for peak experiences, and for excelling. The Dani of course know the difference in size between two pigs, and can act on this knowledge. But there are no simple ways to say "this is the bigger," or to ask "who has the most?" (I would try to ask about such things, of course, and would often get unintentionally misleading answers.) These difficulties are consistent with Dani balance or egalitarianism

and their lack of concern with comparative/competition or superlative/ peaks.

A word of caution, however: All of these are only suggestive similarities between features of Dani language and patterns of Dani culture. We cannot say that any particular linguistic feature necessarily occurs with any particular cultural feature, but at least we can point to these Dani correspondences.

The Dani Past

In one sense the written history of any Dani group goes back to the first expedition which contacted them in 1909 (and the Grand Valley was not discovered by Europeans for another 30 years after that). From those early expedition records we learn little more of historical interest than that the Dani have been living in the same places and doing the same things for at least this century.

There has still been no archaeology reported from the Grand Valley, and so we do not know how long people have been there. Archaeologists who have been working in the highlands of eastern New Guinea report surprisingly early dates for human occupation. According to White (1972:147), people were at least visiting the highlands by about 24,000 B.C.; there was regular occupation by 9000 B.C.; and there is what may be indirect evidence for horticulture and domestic pigs by 7000 B.C. (see Golson 1977:613). But even in the eastern highlands there are many questions to be answered, and in any case, those sites are some 800 kilometers (500 miles) east of the Grand Valley. But it would not be at all surprising if people had known the Grand Valley for a thousand years or more.

A hypothetical reconstruction of Dani prehistory is that they once lived in the lower mountains, hunting birds and marsupials, preparing flour from the wild sago palms, and perhaps sometimes venturing above the sago limit into the Grand Valley. Then they obtained domestic plants like banana, sweet potato, taro, and yams which would grow at higher altitudes, and they were able to occupy the Grand Valley and other farmable valleys around the 1600-meter (5200-foot) altitude level.

The Dani have no direct account of the coming of crops or their shifts from foraging to horticulture, but there is a tantalizing hint in the food of the boys' initiation ceremony (see p. 151). During their four-day seclusion, the initiates are fed only taro, no sweet potatoes. Then at the end of the ceremony the boys get an entire meal of hunted and gathered foods: mice, birds, bees and beehives, crayfish, grasshoppers, wild greens, sweet potato leaves, and pork from a wild pig (see Heider 1972:193). Except for the sweet potato leaves, and possibly the wild pig, every item is prehorticulture. It looks like an ancient memory, preserved in ritual, of the pre-Dani past.

But it is not yet possible to say when the first Dani, or pre-Dani, arrived in the Grand Valley, and when they began to farm the Grand Valley. The first observations of the Grand Valley, made in 1938 (Archbold 1941), showed that the garden ditch system was already extensive. But how long did it take them to clear and shape the land?

There are also hints to suggest that the Dani have not yet fully completed the transition from mobile, scattered hunting and gathering groups to permanent settled horticulture life (see Heider 1967a). Knowing this helps to make sense of some of the present Dani traits like their casual attitude toward land ownership and their frequent movements from compound to compound. But we still do not know how long ago the transformation was begun.

THE DANI ENVIRONMENT

The Grand Valley is a remarkably temperate place to live. There are few extremes of anything, and little variation. Even the landscape is so. The valley floor stretches out in a great broad plain, broken only by a few hills. From these hills, or from the slopes flanking the valley, one can easily command a view of the entire valley, some 45 kilometers (28 miles) from top to bottom and up to 15 kilometers (9 miles) broad. The surrounding mountains reach high above the valley floor and are visible from all parts of the Grand Valley. It is an open land, covered with grass and patches of forests, hard to get lost in. But on the slopes of the valley wall are thick forests of mixed hardwoods and a few remnant araucaria pines.

The combination of altitude, latitude, and mountains protects the valley from any great seasonal changes. At 4° south of the Equator the Grand Valley is within the tropics, but at 1600 meters (5200 feet) it is high above the steamy heat of coastal New Guinea, and the 3000-meter (9800-foot) mountains effectively shield it from monsoons.

Rainfall is moderate. There are about 2000 millimeters (78 inches) per year, fairly evenly distributed throughout the year, although in most years there is more rain in February and March than in other months. There are irregular wet spells and dry spells, but the Dani recognized no regular yearly seasonal cycle. The mean range of temperature is from 26°C (78.8°F) to about 15°C (59°F), with extremes at 29.5°C (85°F) to 6°C (42°F).

Every few years the Balim River overflows its banks, flooding some sweet potato fields. I have heard stories of people having to harvest their sweet potatoes from rafts floating across the fields. But these floods do no permanent damage. The area where we lived is so far from the river that it is spared even this mild problem.

There is no dangerous wildlife. The nearby forests have been nearly hunted out and even cassowary birds and feral pigs, which roam elsewhere in the highlands, are unknown in the Grand Valley.

The land itself is reasonably fertile, but no valuable minerals have been discovered in the Grand Valley. This will prove to be another mixed blessing to the Dani in the future.

It is tempting to say that the temperateness of the Dani environment contributes to the temperate pattern of Dani culture, but that would be taking environmentalism too far. At least two other groups in the New Guinea Highlands—the Egaki (Pospisil 1963:81) and the Huli (Glasse 1968:19)—have very similar climates but quite different cultures. Therefore, it is obvious that lack of seasons alone is not an overwhelming causal factor. So one falls back to a much weaker statement: In some respects the Dani environment is consistent with Dani culture, and the environment may be one of many factors in a complex causal fabric which acts to shape Dani culture.

We can mention other ways in which the environment interacts with the culture. The daytime mildness means that the Dani do not have to develop warm clothing, and they solve the problem of night chill with snug sleeping lofts in their houses. The lack of real seasons means that sweet potatoes can be grown and harvested the year round. Once they are dug up, sweet potatoes do not store well, but in the Grand Valley this is not a problem, and this one crop can be the year-round single food staple.

Because of the altitude and isolation, the Grand Valley has been a remarkably healthful place. The worst diseases were yaws and minor respiratory ailments.

But despite the temperateness of the climate, the Grand Valley is just within the upper range of such tropical plants as banana and pandanus, so the Dani get the benefits of several ecological zones.

This, then, is what I mean by calling the Dani environment "temperate": It provides no strong challenge or extreme conditions; the Dani have adapted to what is surely one of the most benign and permissive of human habitats.

DANI SUBSISTENCE TECHNOLOGY

Food

The Dani are overwhelmingly a pork and sweet potato people. Something like 90 percent of their diet is sweet potato, steamed or baked. The other 10 percent is made up of a great variety of foods, almost all of which they grow themselves.

Most of the meat they eat comes from their domestic pigs, which are killed only at ceremonial occasions. But there are enough pigs and enough ceremonies so that most people get a few ounces of pork every week or so.

There are other minor root crops like taro and yam; there are lots of banana plants around every compound, but the fruit takes so long to mature at this altitude that banana is not an important food. People grow sugar cane and cucumber for snacks, and plenty of greens are used in the steam bundles—sweet potato leaves, especially, but also various other leaves which ethnographers always call "spinach-like." If there is a delicacy, it would be the various sorts of pandanus. One kind has a great long red fruit which is steamed and squeezed out to make a strong red paste which flavors other foods. Another kind of pandanus tree bears nuts. These are baked, the tough shells smashed open, and the savory little meats picked out and eaten.

The Dani are certainly not gourmets. There is little variety in cooking or in menu. The only seasonings are the red pandanus paste, ginger roots, or salt. The interest or importance of food for the Dani lies not in the ingenuity of the recipe or the elegance of the service, but in the meaning of the gathering. Ceremonies of all sorts involve cooking masses of simple food for many people to eat and take away.

But despite the overwhelming preponderance of sweet potato in their diet, the Dani are obviously well-nourished, healthy, active people. I am still surprised at how healthy the sweet potato is, and I anticipate trouble in the future as the Dani become more integrated into Indonesian culture. For most Indonesians, rice is the proper food and the sweet potato has very low status indeed. But since the Dani cannot grow rice, it would be both economically and nutritionally disastrous if they were drawn into a rice diet.

Hunting and Gathering

Although most Dani will grab a handful of berries to munch on, and boys often take potshots at birds, hunting and gathering is now almost inconsequential in providing food. A few men who like hunting live at the edge of the forest, keep dogs, and go after marsupials, but most do not bother. Children sometimes catch crayfish but until the Dutch began stocking ponds and streams in the 1960s, there were no fish at all in the Grand Valley waters.

Pigs

Pigs are everywhere. Every Dani household keeps pigs, which are about as numerous as people. The largest structures which the Dani build are the pig sties. They open onto the courtyards and shelter pigs whenever they are not wandering in the courtyard or being herded outside. Pigs often scavenge in the courtyards, cleaning up garbage from meals and leaving their own feces in turn. Dani home life is marked by the smell of pigs and the sound of pigs as they grunt and bang at the loose stall boards day and night, and Dani ceremonies are marked by their squeals as they die.

Pigs are an important part of a Dani's experience. They are the first creatures which a child gets to know on an eye-to-eye basis. Pigs have names, and while not exactly affectionate, are always around. Since these pigs which grow up in the compound are then routinely killed, butchered, and eaten there, it is inevitable that Dani children learn from these experiences about the naturalness of death.

Rappaport, in his valuable ecological study of the Maring in eastern New Guinea, called attention to the complex role which pigs play in energy exchanges of the subsistence technology (1967). Pigs convert carbohydrates

Hagigake, a two-year-old, helps one of the women of her compound herd pigs out to the grazing grounds. The anthropologist's house is in the background.

to protein, but since the Maring need to raise food for the pigs, that protein has a very high cost. In energy terms alone, Maring pigs may not be worth it. However, the Dani pigs live almost exclusively off waste. They eat garbage in the compounds and the last small tubers in a field after the women have harvested it out. They also spend lots of time rooting for small things in old fallow garden areas. Dani children under the age of 10 years are given responsibility for watching over the family herd in the fields and forests.

The other major cost of Dani pigs lies in their high potential for causing serious trouble. This problem is real, but hard to measure. Pigs are easily stolen. Sometimes they actually are, and sometimes when one is merely lost or strayed, the owner assumes that it has been stolen and looks for the thief. Pig thefts within a group can usually be smoothed over, often with payment of a couple of pigs in restitution. But thefts across confederation or alliance boundaries more usually contribute to tension which can eventually burst out in warfare. (The costs and benefits of Dani pigs are summarized in Diagram 1.)

Costs	Benefits
some minor food production done especially for the pigs	food: everything edible is eaten
constant herding supervision (mainly young children)	blood: eaten or used in magic
construction and maintenance of sties	tusks: scrapers, nose ornaments
	mandibles: part of ritual treasure
easily stolen or strayed, so source of much conflict	long bones: needles, awls
	ribs: scrape baked potatoes
	ilium: spoon
feces possible source of disease (?)	can be traded to Jalé for fine forest products
	great importance in ritual exchanges

Diagram 1. The Dani pig, embedded. The costs and benefits which result from the Dani pig industry.

The benefits of pigs are many. Virtually every edible part is eaten. The blood is used to smear magical signs on people or things; tails are used as ornaments; the scrotum and penis of the male pig is carefully removed and used as an arm band to ward off ghosts. Bones and teeth are made into a variety of tools. Pigs raised in the Grand Valley are often taken to the Jalémo, where they are traded for forest products like furs, feathers, and fine woods. Unless they could figure out some way to milk, ride, or plow with pigs, it is hard to imagine how the Dani could use their pigs more fully.

But in a deeper sense it is the remembrance of pigs which holds Dani society together. At every major ceremony pigs are given from one person to another, and then killed and eaten. But they leave behind memory traces of obligations which will be paid back later; when this happens, the people will create new obligations. And so the network of the society is constantly refurbished by the passage of pigs. A single man in his lifetime is bound to his fellows by the ties of hundreds and perhaps thousands of pigs which he and his people have exchanged with others and their people.

Finally, the Dani do not just house and feed pigs. They breed them selectively, castrating most males. They say that a castrated male will grow fat, have larger tusks, and not run after female pigs, and they are right. They tend to their pigs' wounds; every so often pigs would emerge from their stalls in the morning with wounds which the Dani attribute to mice or rats. If shoats have become motherless too early, they are carefully fed with special food. However, I have never seen a Dani woman nursing a pig on her own breast, as occurs in the eastern highlands (Mervyn Meggit, personal communication). The Dani seem to have made a discovery about female pigs which I have been unable to explain. Several times I have seen a man take a young female pig, make incisions in its belly, pull out a whitish cord, sever it, push the ends back into the cut, and patch the wound. They say that they do it to make the pig grow, and that it does not effect its reproductive powers. Since they have a scientifically acceptable understanding of castration, it is hard to believe that this operation is not also rational. But I have not been able to find anyone who can explain what it does for the pig.

Sweet Potatoes

Pigs go everywhere, but sweet potatoes grow everywhere. In all, the Dani cultivate at least 14 different species of plants, including tobacco and the gourds which make water jugs and penis gourds. But of all these, sweet potato is by far the most important in terms of its food value, the amount of land devoted to it, and the energy put into it.

Most groups in the New Guinea highlands are similarly specialized in sweet potatoes, but it is fair to say that none has as sophisticated a cultivation technology as the Grand Valley Dani. In 1961 the botanist Chris Versteegh, then with the Dutch government experimental agricultural station in Manokwari, paid us a visit. He kept exclaiming over the Dani sweet potato plantings and said that it was far in advance of what they were doing with sweet potatoes at Manokwari.

There are three sorts of gardens: Most crops are raised in the long fallow permanent garden system on the valley floor; some men have gardens on the mountain slopes which they clear, burn off, and plant for a growing cycle or two; and everyone plants tobacco, sugar cane, and bananas in their compound, behind the houses.

Throughout the Grand Valley one sees the elaborate ditch system of the sweet potato gardens. The ditches are certainly old, but we have no idea when or even why they were dug. Perhaps at first they were necessary to

Air view of partially planted sweet potato gardens. A small compound is being built at the edge of the fallow area.

Air view of new sweet potato gardens. The mounds indicate areas which have been planted, but note the irregular planting pattern (see p. 42).

drain swampy areas, and then when their other advantages were understood, they were used wherever possible. The ditches are multifunctional:

1. When it rains too much, they drain water away from the sweet potato tubers in the high-standing garden beds and prevent rotting.

2. The ditches also serve as extensions of the natural stream patterns of an area so that during dry spells they can channel water through the garden beds.

3. The ditches protect the gardens from marauding pigs. Many garden areas are accessible only by single-pole bridges thrown across the moatlike ditches. (These are impossible for pigs and, when muddy, nearly so for anthropologists.) Other gardens can be closed off with short fences across narrow necks of land. The Dani are thus spared the time-consuming fence building which occupies most people who try to grow crops and livestock simultaneously.

4. Most important, these ditches serve as mulching basins. Topsoil washes off and collects in them; when women weed and prune the sweet potato vines, they toss the trash into the ditches. So for an entire growing period as the topside beds are being cultivated, the ditch bottoms are being enriched. Then at the beginning of the next planting, this rich mud is scooped up and slopped over the beds, ensuring the continued productivity of the soil.

The valley floor gardens are worked in a fallow garden cycle with several set steps:

1. The land is cleared. If it has been fallow only a short time, it may be covered in grass and weeds. Later, small scrub trees which the Dani call *pabi* (it also means "feces" and "incest") will establish themselves. The men clear everything with digging sticks and stone adzes, let it dry for a few days, and then burn it. The ashes dissolve in to nourish the soil.

2. The sod is broken and turned by men using the heavy pole digging sticks.

3. Ditch mud is spread over the garden beds. This opens up the ditches and also revitalizes the gardens.

4. Now the women come for the planting. First they stop off at a more advanced garden and collect cuttings from older sweet potato vines. At the new garden they make lines of regular low mounds and plant the vines, two to a mound.

5. For the next six months or so the women will pay only an occasional visit to that garden to keep up on the weeding, to turn the vines to the sun, and to take cuttings for new gardens elsewhere.

6. Harvesting begins about six months after planting, and it continues for about three months. A woman goes to her mature garden every day and digs up just enough sweet potatoes for her family's immediate needs.

7. When there are no more good-sized tubers to be found, pigs will be brought in to root after the last small tubers, to churn up the soil, and to contribute their droppings to its fertilization. Then the land lies fallow as grass, bushes, and trees begin to cover it, and the next cycle is ready to begin.

I suppose that I spent more time to less advantage on gardening than any other single subject. It did not take long to work out the general steps outlined above. But that left many questions: What are the work patterns? When does a man work alone when in a big cooperative work party? Who owns land? How are rights transferred? How long is land left fallow? What is the productivity of land? I was hoping for precise answers but in the end I was happy with a few vague ones. The Dani work sporadically on any one garden bed, and in the course of a day a person will visit and work on several different beds at different stages of maturity.

Elsewhere in New Guinea, where the sweet potato gardens are rectangular, the culture quantitative, and the people cooperative, an anthropologist can send boys out to pace off the garden areas, have women bring their harvest by to be weighed, and wind up with good production statistics. This approach was just not possible with the Dani.

Dani fields are very irregular, and it was hard to map, much less measure, land area. With aerial photographs I made up a set of maps and walked all the gardens in the neighborhood regularly to record what was going on. Little activity followed a rigid pattern. Planting even in a small area would be staggered over days or weeks and then the harvesting would be spread over months. (This practice is obviously an advantage when one wishes to harvest every day and have a field yield as long as possible.) Some plots were immediately recycled; others lay fallow for months or years. It looks as if the fertilization system is so effective that with care the fallow period is not even necessary. Households have several fields at different stages in widely separated areas. In theory one could say that this is insurance against a disease in one spot destroying the entire food supply, but in fact I never saw

From a sheltered platform atop a watchtower a man looks over newly planted sweet potato gardens, scanning the no-man's-land for signs of an enemy raiding party.

evidence that that was a danger. There may be a more important effect of scattering the plots (although the Dani may not be consciously planning it): It gives everyone a chance to have social ties and cooperative work parties with several different sets of neighbors.

It is better to speak of usage rights than land ownership. If a man wants to open a garden, he will ask other people in the neighborhood and the man who last farmed that plot, and then he will use it without compensating anyone. As long as there is plenty of land, the system works well and allows maximum flexibility. But the well-being of the people is very vulnerable under this system, and it would be easy for outsiders to come in, establish new rules, "buy" land from some Dani, and permanently alienate it from the Dani horticultural system.

Other Crops

The sweet potato is very much the year-round staple crop and foodstuff, but there are several other crops worthy of note. The two other tubers are taro and yams, both fairly uncommon. Taro is an essential element in the boys' initiation ceremony, held every five or 10 years, but it is rarely eaten otherwise. Compared to the succulent sweet potato, it has all the appeal of boiled cotton. I have the feeling that the only reason the Dani keep taro going at all is to be able to have large quantities for the ceremony. (My colleagues who have worked elsewhere in Melanesia insist that taro grown at sea level is delicious.)

Every man raises tobacco, usually near his compound, and all adult Dani smoke cigarettes made of a tiny bit of this home-grown tobacco rolled in the leaf of a wild spurge. At the time I was doing fieldwork, I smoked heavily myself, and once tried a pipe-full of Dani tobacco. It was so strong that it made me seriously ill for half a day.

Certainly the most important of these minor crops is the banana. Bananas are planted around every compound, and the sound of their great leaves blowing in the wind is part of the Dani atmosphere. As I mentioned before, the Grand Valley is about at the upper limit of banana cultivation. On the coast it takes only a few months for banana plants to bear their stalks of fruit. Here it takes two years. In addition, bananas are usually cut down while still green to save them from the fruit bats and flying foxes which come flapping through the night to feast on the ripe fruit. I counted 16 varieties of bananas, some of which are quite delicious. But banana plants serve so many other uses that the fruit is almost a minor by-product. The tall plant (which, since its stalks are not woody, is not called a tree) shelters the compounds from sun and wind. The leaves are used for wrapping food, and the outer sheaves of the bark dry into a tough soft substance which is used to wrap all manner of things. The layers of the stalk are used in making salt. First they are dried and then carried to the brine pool where they are soaked and squeezed until they are full of the salty liquid. Then, after being dried again they are burned and the resulting ash, rich in salt and other minerals,

Women soaking up salty liquid in dried banana bark at the Iluekainma, the major brine pool in the Dani region.

is made into a ball, wrapped in banana bark, and sprinkled on food laid out on banana leaves.

But despite the tremendous skills which the Grand Valley Dani brought to their horticulture, they are quite conservative. Although the missionaries tried for years, they did not get the Dani to accept new vegetables, and even when they did it was to have a small cash crop, rather than to vary their own diet. This is in great contrast to the Western Dani, who had taken up maize in the 1930s or 1940s, ahead of any direct European contact, and who by 1970 were growing huge amounts of all manner of newly introduced foods.

DENSITY OF POPULATION

The Grand Valley Dani have one of the highest densities of population in New Guinea. It may be two or three times that of most other highland groups (Brown and Podolefsky 1976). Brookfield, in his study of Melanesian cultivation, rates the Dani as having the highest density of cultivation in New

Guinea (1971:106). Unfortunately, we have only approximate figures for both population and territory. If we figure the Grand Valley to be about 45 kilometers long and 15 kilometers wide at its widest, with a total area of about 315 square kilometers, and if the population is about 50,000, then the population density is about 160 people per square kilometer (or 440 per square mile). The Dugum Neighborhood, with about 350 people in about two square kilometers, has a population density of about 175 people per square kilometer (or 454 per square mile) (see Heider 1970:59–60).

But we must be wary of these figures for the Grand Valley. Of course, it will be much better when we have an accurate land survey as well as good census figures. But even then, the Grand Valley settlements are different from much of the rest of the New Guinea highlands. In theoretical terms we can speak in a rough way of three sorts of land use: residential, horticultural, and forest. Now, for example, to compare the density of Manhattan with that of South Carolina is obviously misleading for some purposes because the South Carolina land includes both dwelling and farms, while the New York figures leave out the farmland which provides food for Manhattanites. The figure for the Grand Valley land includes only residential and horticultural land, but not the extensive forests which stretch up the flanking hills and out beyond the valley. In other parts of New Guinea, one finds the people, their gardens, and their forests all together in a single valley. So, in figuring the total land area for them, we would be including a type of land—forests— that is not included in the Grand Valley figure. And of course, although forests are not intensively exploited by any New Guinea highland peoples, they are important for firewood, lumber, vines, and other wild products.

Therefore, perhaps the Grand Valley density figures should not be compared directly with other New Guinea highland population density figures for the economic purpose of telling us how much land the people use. But the figures are still accurate in the social sense, for they indicate how much denser the population on the Grand Valley floor is than elsewhere in the highlands.

But what do these figures mean? In comparison with East African cattle herders who can have population densities about 10 people per square kilometer, or hunters and gatherers with several square kilometers per person, the Grand Valley seems impossibly overpopulated; but in comparison with intensely irrigated rice regions of Japan or Java, where the population density can be 2000 people per square kilometer, the Grand Valley is practically deserted. What is important is that with the Grand Valley Dani we find no evidence of overpopulation. This concept of overpopulation, the idea that a population can expand toward some physical limit, is familiar today. But although we can talk about the future population problems of the planet, it is difficult to apply this same concept to the Dani. In eastern New Guinea there are groups which suffer from overpopulation with a quarter the density of the Dani. But overpopulation is a complex total of land factors, technological factors, social factors, and psychological attitudes. In any case, there is no reason to think that the Dani are pushing their population limits. Much land in the valley floor is not occupied, or is in a very long-term fallow state. Because Dani horticulture does not seem to wear out the soil, it seems likely that the productivity of the land could be intensified without ill effects. Their population pattern is also influenced by the fact that most Dani are gregarious and enjoy living in close large settlements.

No Dani behavior is easily attributable to any sort of population squeeze. In extreme instances one alliance routs another and takes over its land. But even such a case is not a solution to population pressure since it is the stronger group, not necessarily the more densely populated group, which is the victor.

We can point to a few correlates of the dense population. Dani households consume quantities of firewood for cooking and for warmth. If the population were to increase, the forest of the valley floor could become depleted, creating a hardship especially for the people living along the Balim River in the center of the Grand Valley. But people like the Gutelu, at the edge of the valley, have endless forests at their backs, and would be less affected. Already the valley floor has been hunted out. In all my time there I saw only one bird-of-paradise, no cassowaries, and no marsupials. Dani covet the feathers and furs from these creatures for ornaments, and to get them now they must maintain trade relations with the Jalé people, several days' walk through the forests. (At least this is a good way for the Jalé to acquire salt and pigs from the Grand Valley.) Otherwise there is no sign that the resources of the Grand Valley are being depleted by population pressure.

It is interesting to speculate about the social implications of the population density. Not only are there more people closer together than elsewhere in the highlands, but the flat valley floor makes travel much easier than elsewhere. So in terms of actual potential for human interaction, the Grand Valley Dani are much closer to each other than even the population figures indicate. But they also have less in-group conflict and violence than most other New Guinea groups. The Grand Valley alliances, with about 5000 people each, are larger political units than most highland cultures have, but even here the dense population is not very significant. The people of the alliance rarely convene. At most, one can say an effect of this population density is that hundreds of fighting men can reach the site of a battle within a couple of hours.

In summary, then, the Dani's sophisticated intense horticulture allows exceptionally high population density in the Grand Valley without strains of overpopulation or apparently many other effects on Dani life.

LABOR AND ITS DIVISION

Dani division of labor is quite simple. There are no full-time or even part-time specialists. There is some specialization by age, of course. Children begin to participate in work as soon as they can walk, but they do not take a full share of work until their midteens. There is some specialization by sex also. Men do the heavy work in the gardens and house building, and are much more involved in politics, ritual affairs, and of course warfare. Women do the long, tedious work. In the gardens they do most of the planting, weeding, and harvesting, as well as the cooking; they have most responsibility for herding the pigs and tending the children. Nearly all the women lack two to six fingers, which were chopped off for funeral sacrifices when they were girls (see p. 133). But surprisingly this does not hinder their work. They even roll the string and make the carrying nets. However, it is the men who do the finest handicraft work like knitting the shell bands for funerals.

The fact is, though, that the Dani economy does not demand much work from anyone. Even the women, who spend more actual hours working, usually have plenty of time to sit around their hearths and talk. Men's work is done more in spurts. When building a house or opening a new garden, men will work steadily through several days. Ceremonies also usually occupy all of a day or two, but little of this time is really spent in labor. Battles, likewise, take a day. However, most of the men's days are spent sitting, visiting, gossiping, perhaps idly knitting on a shell band. The Dani are not like people at the mercy of a short growing season and capricious weather who need to store up huge surpluses of food to last them through the lean season or to ensure against an unpredictable disaster. And their material tastes are simple. They do not invest time, energy, and wealth in public works, great buildings, or great art. They do not invest extra energy in much at all. Their artifacts and technologies are ingeniously practical, but rarely is energy spent adding beauty to a thing.

I was always surprised at how little the Dani valued my artifacts. Steel knives, machetes, shovels, and axes rarely roused much interest. Most Dani, it seemed, felt that they could say no to an offer of trade goods. If someone worked for me, or helped me with my research, it was very much at their pleasure and whim. This sort of attitude of course drives outsiders to despair over the "lazy shiftless natives who just won't work." The solution, which many outsiders are working on, is to make the Dani covet cotton clothes, rice, flashlight batteries, or other such things which can be bought only by extra labor.

The Dani have been remarkably self-sufficient. Each nuclear family can grow its own food, and provide its own shelter. Groups of men, friends, and neighbors often get together in a cooperative work party to begin on a new garden area or to build a house—but this is to make the task more entertaining. Each man will be doing the same thing, and the work will be merely the sum total of all the workers. There are very few tasks which need more than one or two people to manage. Most tasks are like mudding the gardens. Ten men can slop 10 times as much mud, and have more fun doing it, than one man can, but mudding is essentially a one-man job. This is another aspect of lack of specialization, in this case seen in the arrangements of routine tasks rather than long-term roles. In a similar lack of specialization, the social exchange networks are created by the gifts of pigs and shells. But of course, pigs and shells are things which everyone has, not scarce products of specialization which everyone needs. Thus, exchanging such shared goods is a dramatic affirmation of the social rather than economic basis for gift exchange at Dani ceremonies (see p. 144).

Circulation of Goods

With this minimal division of labor, there is little need for circulation of goods, but one can point to three main spheres of circulation: family consumption, ceremonies, and outright trade.

The first, most basic, sphere consists of those vegetables, and especially sweet potatoes, which are grown, cooked, and eaten within the family at normal meals.

Ceremonies are occasions for much movement of goods: People bring pigs and sweet potatoes which are cooked and then distributed to everyone. Valuable symbolic goods like cowrie shell bands, nets, and skirting are brought by some and redistributed to others by the leader of the ceremony after he confers with others present.

Outright trade is carried on for imported goods like adze stones, exchange stones, fine furs, feathers, and wood in exchange for goods like salt, pigs, and nets which are produced in the Grand Valley. Small groups of men make trading trips between the Grand Valley and neighboring populations. Although there are no regular traders among the Grand Valley Dani, some men are especially fond of making such trips.

SETTLEMENTS

The Compound

The basic Dani settlement is the compound in which at least one nuclear family lives. A compound consists of four essential structures: a round men's house, a smaller round women's house, a rectangular cook house, and a rectangular pig sty. These buildings all open onto a common courtyard with the men's house at one end facing the compound's entrance at the other. The buildings are joined by short fence segments so that the courtyard is completely enclosed. A second outer fence surrounds the entire compound.

Anywhere from three to a couple of dozen people live in a single compound. The basic plan is constant, but with more people there are more women's houses, the cook house is longer and has more hearths, and the pig sties are longer with more stalls (see Diagram 2).

The people in one compound are friends and often they are related families. In most compounds there is a Big Man, one who is more important than the others, and the others are there because of their links to him. But

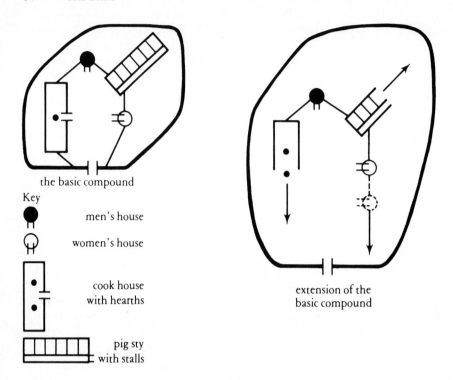

the basic compound

Key

● men's house

Ⓗ women's house

cook house
with hearths

pig sty
with stalls

extension of the
basic compound

Diagram 2.   Plan of settlements.

since every Dani is related to every other Dani in some way or another, kinship per se is not nearly as strong a determining factor as is friendship. As friendships wax and wane people move.

In my first months with the Dani I tried to make an accurate census of the Dugum Neighborhood, but I was always frustrated by the Dani pattern of movement. For an apparently settled people they have remarkably high residential mobility. Rarely would any but the smallest compound have the same population two months in a row. But most of this movement was confined to the Neighborhood, and the Neighborhood itself has a more stable population. There are many reasons for a Dani to move from one compound to another: to avoid friction with others, to move a pig herd closer to fresh rooting grounds, or to be closer to a new garden area. But for the Dani such moves were routine and unremarkable.

The 350 people of the Dugum Neighborhood lived in a total of 35 compounds during 1961–1963, but at any one moment no more than 30 compounds were actually occupied. Often families would maintain houses and hearths in two compounds. One would be in an older settled place and one at the forest edge or near a temporary quiet frontier. I estimated that there are about twice as many houses standing as were actually in use. This occupancy pattern is part of the great flexibility in Dani social relationships.

Air view directly down on three compound clusters of the Dugum Neighborhood: Wubakainma, Homaklep, and Abugulmo. Wubakainma, on the left, has four compounds and the anthropologist's house. The regular rectangular plots of a current slope garden are visible just above Homaklep. The gardens below Homaklep were fallow and covered with small trees when the photograph was taken in 1964, but by 1970 this area was cleared and again under cultivation.

But I often thought how it would mislead someone doing an aerial survey or, in the future, an archaeological reconstruction.

The Compound Cluster

Of those 35 compounds in the Dugum Neighborhood, only eight stood isolated, apart from another compound. They were the pioneer compounds, usually fairly temporary settlements which had been built at the edges of the Neighborhood. All the rest of the compounds were clumped together in groups ranging from two to five compounds. In such groups, adjacent compounds shared an inner fence, and a single fence enclosed the entire settlement area.

At first I was tempted to call these larger units "hamlets" or even "villages." At Wubakainma, for instance, there were four compounds (in addition to the abandoned fifth one where I had built my own house) where about 50 people lived within the outer fence. Elsewhere in the Grand Valley

Men thatch a cook house.

there were even larger settlements. Gutelu's place at Jibiga had some dozen compounds with well over 100 people most of the time.

But despite size and appearance, these large concentrations of people are not villages. They are geographical concentrations of people but they are not social units. They are simply accretions of compounds. I finally decided to call them "compound clusters." Each compound is a recognizable social group. However temporary, it does have leaders and ties among its members. But there is no leadership or other organization for the compound cluster, and any one compound in a cluster is as likely to have its closest ties with people in another cluster as with people over the fence. The compound cluster is analogous to a residential block in an American city, where one probably has more interaction with friends and relatives across town than with next door neighbors.

These compound clusters, then, give a false impression of the sociopolitical organization of the Grand Valley Dani. They would suggest to our hypothetical aerial photographer or archaeologist a complex village organization. In fact, the compound cluster is only the sum of the individual compounds, no more. This organization is analogous to the Dani work pattern, where the larger work parties or the extensive ditch systems suggest considerably more sociopolitical organization than actually exists. The Dani are a fine case of Durkheim's mechanical solidarity, where considerable size is achieved by the accumulation of like units rather than of functionally specialized units.

The older and larger compounds are spread out along the edge of the valley with easy access to the forest behind, within sight of each other, and with their sweet potato gardens stretching out in front of them toward the frontier, forming a zone of security in time of war. From one compound cluster one can see the banana grove hiding the next, and in the early mornings and late afternoons the blue smoke of the cooking fires rises from each settlement.

Dani days begin and end in the compound. Women, girls, and younger boys sleep in the women's houses. Sometimes a woman has her own house, but more often she shares it with another woman—co-wife, her mother, or her mother-in-law. But this arrangement is socially unstable, for if there is any friction between the women—and there often is—one will move out, usually to another compound. However, women spend more time in the common cook house, a long rectangular structure with cooking hearths down the center of it. Each woman has her own hearth where she can sit working on her nets, receiving visitors, and baking sweet potatoes. Often a small piglet or two is tethered to a center post. The cook house is a lively place, where women gossip from hearth to hearth and where the families gather.

Most men spend most of their nights in the men's house, although a few men do sleep regularly with their wives and the rest may visit theirs for an occasional night. But the men usually stay in the men's house rather than in the cook house. Although there are no real sexual antagonisms here (certainly not compared with other Highlands groups), the men's houses are for males only. Little girls who come with their fathers are welcomed up to the age of about five or six.

In the house the men sit around the central hearth talking, knitting, working on ornaments, or most often just smoking and gossiping. This continual gossip by men and women is not often vicious, personally derogatory tales, but just trivial chatter about nothing special. Malinowski long ago pointed out that such language served more for social bonding than for actual communication of information. Sometimes there are long lulls in the talk. Someone will strum on a bamboo mouth harp. Occasionally, one hears a quite extraordinary noise of a man grinding his teeth. This is not done in anger, however; in fact, if it communicates anything, it is quiet contentment. A fire usually smolders in the hearth during the day for warmth or at least for lighting cigarettes. Men often lie down on the soft grass floor or crawl upstairs into the sleeping loft to take a nap. The men's house also serves as a workshop. Its walls are lined with packages of all sizes: feathers, furs, shells, string, gourds, and ornaments in all stages of completion. In the more important men's houses the sacred stones of a sib are stored in a sort of wall cupboard at the rear of the room.

The Dani day begins after dawn as people begin to stir in the compound. Someone crawls down to stoke up the fires which have been banked over in the men's house and the cook house. Sweet potatoes are put in the coals to bake, and people have their first cigarettes. Pigs may be let out of their sties to forage around in the courtyard. It usually takes a couple of hours for the sun to burn away the morning fog, and Dani rarely move out of their compounds early.

By midmorning, however, the compounds are deserted and quiet, for the Dani and their pigs have spread out to begin their day's work or visiting. Within a few hours people begin to drift home with bundles of firewood, nets of newly harvested and washed sweet potatoes, perhaps cigarette leaves collected from the forest, or if nothing tangible, at least information about the doings in the Neighborhood.

By late afternoon, women have started baking the evening meal, the pigs are barred back into the sties for the night, and the compounds settle down to eat, talk, and eventually go to sleep. There are no specific times for retiring, and children seem to stay up as late as adults. Only rarely do Dani leave the compounds at night except when the moon is full and the sky is clear. Then children and teenagers play noisily in the moonlit forests and fields until early in the morning, and everyone sleeps a little later the next day.

Making Houses

The Dani men's house nicely expresses both environmental adaptation and Dani character. The environment is regularly chilly, often rainy, and contains mosquitoes; at the same time it provides plentiful wood and grass.

The men's and women's houses (they are built to similar plans) have thick thatched roofs which keep out rain, yet retain the heat from the hearth, along with just enough smoke to discourage the mosquitoes. The house does provide these essential protections but it does little more. In line with the pattern of Dani culture, the house is not intellectualized; that is, it is not elaborate in size, form, or decoration beyond the basics. The house is made of broad planks and poles which are casually cut and lashed together. Practically nothing in the house is really carpentered or cut to fit, yet it all holds together well. Even the gaps between the wall slats of the lower room have a function, for they help to keep that room reasonably smoke-free.

It takes a couple of weeks to make a house. The men of the compound begin by gathering lumber, poles, and vines. They may salvage the sound wood from an old abandoned house, or they may go into the forest to cut new wood. When everything is collected they start construction. Often friends drop by to help a bit. Work goes sporadically. Men often take breaks to attend a ceremony, work in a garden, or wait out a rainy day at home. The last stage is thatching, which is done in one day, always with help from other men and, for the first time, from women. Men go out to a fallow garden which has grown high with grass. They pluck the grass and tie it into large bundles which women and girls carry on their heads to the house site. Then some men toss the bundles up to others standing on the roof, and it is skillfully built into a watertight, windproof grass roof.

Holism and the Men's House

At one point the Grand Valley Dani houses, particularly the men's house, came under criticism as government officials attempted to force a change in the architecture. One government report put it this way:

> Their housing is extremely poor. Huts are built of tree poles with thatched roof, primitive structures with no attention given to hygienic or aesthetic factors. The people sleep on the floor, on a bedding of grass, around the fireplace for protection against the cold. In actual fact, they are eager to have proper houses like those used by people in other provinces. . . . They are to attain such standards as will enable them to build houses and villages of the type found in other districts, and to keep them in good condition. . . .

The Dani men's house is in any case the most complex and revealing cultural artifact of the Dani, but this government attack focuses attention on it, making it a political issue and a controversial object.

There are many possible kinds of anthropological approaches to understanding the Dani men's house: historical, structural, symbolic, psychological, social, ecological, and so forth. But in response to the government attack, the most effective approach is the holistic one.

Holism is not so much a theory as an assumption that the different features of a culture are more or less interrelated in a total, contextual system. Therefore, to understand a trait—in this case, the men's house—it is necessary to trace out the context, to explore the ways in which the men's house is embedded in Dani culture. Only then can one successfully evaluate it and perhaps recommend changes. Obviously, it would not make sense to take holism to the extreme of saying that everything is totally integrated with everything else in a culture. Its strength as an approach lies in its treatment of culture as a complex rather than as a simple system. For example, the governmental statement quoted above makes two substantive complaints about the men's house: that it is unhygienic and unaesthetic. But it ignores all the other functions or cultural interrelationships, and some of these we can show through a holistic analysis are directly relevant to any change in architecture.

Diagram 3 shows a holistic analysis of the Dani men's house. On the left we see the factors which contribute to the form of the men's house. These inputs, which are causal to varying degrees, can be called *preconditions*. On the right are the many results of the house design. These functions, or outputs, we can call *effects*.

We have already touched on most of the preconditions. For completeness we can now add that ghosts are an ever-present danger to Dani well-being (see pp. 121–123); that both fire and war, often in concert, are at least potential menaces; and that the men's house is concerned with all three.

One can see at a glance the many functions which the men's house serves and the effects which stem from its design. The building is a low, closed, warm, and smoky structure which gives the men protection from cold and mosquitoes. The smoky environment, along with their constant cigarette smoking (although they do not inhale), may also produce lung cancer or

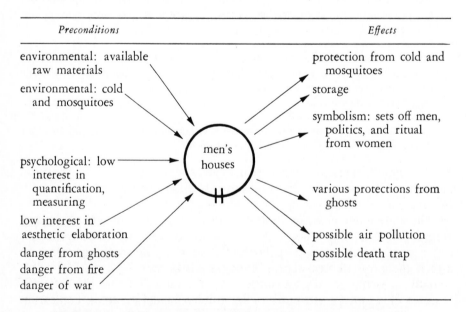

Diagram 3.   Holistic summary of the Dani men's house in context.

related diseases. (That would be an irony, for the Dani are far removed from the factories, traffic, and other polluters of industrialized society.) But here I am only guessing, and this is something which a competent medical researcher should investigate.

The men's house also serves to isolate men from women and to separate women from all the politics, discussions, and rituals which take place there. In many details the men's house protects people from ghosts; it has various features which are meant to intercept and divert any ghosts which might enter.

In case of bad fire or enemy attack, the men's house could well be a death trap, for it has only one entrance and its walls and roofs are too sturdy to break out through. This did happen during the 1966 massacre when attackers set fire to thatched roofs and then waited by the doors, striking down people as they crawled out through the low openings.

These, then, are some of the effects of the Dani men's house. To return to the government complaints against it, we see first that the Dani are not concerned about aesthetics. However, the health factor is more problematical because we lack hard data. In general the Dani seem to be very healthy, and are not suffering from unhygienic living conditions. On the other hand, it is obvious that if one opened up the Dani houses to make them light and airy, one would create other health problems. I built a large open house in Wubakainma, but I had a sleeping bag and mosquito netting. The Dani do not. They keep warm and mosquito-free through the design of their houses. If then their houses are redesigned by governmental fiat, some other solutions for night cold and mosquitoes must be found. In short, this holistic analysis helps us to understand the men's house, and to point out that while one could alter the design, there would be certain predictable consequences.

DANI TOOLS

The presence of stone-bladed tools in a culture makes it almost obligatory that the culture be called "Stone Age." So be it. In 1961 most Dani were still using their own traditional tools with cutting edges made of stone, bone, wood, and bamboo. A decade later most people had steel axes and machetes, but the old tool kits were still around and often used.

Stone Adzes and Axes

Oval stone blades ground down to an edge are traded in to the Grand Valley from distant quarries and then hafted by their Grand Valley owners. The stones then are common throughout the Dani region, but the style of hafting varies from place to place. Since the Grand Valley Dani did not actually manufacture their own blades, they were always dependent on trade routes. These stone blades were the one essential item of their economy in which they were not self-sufficient.

In the Grand Valley, stone axes were used for splitting wood.

In the Grand Valley both adzes (with cutting edge at right angles to the handle) and axes (with cutting edges parallel to the handle) were used. But adzes were far more popular, and they outnumbered the axes by five or 10 to one. Adzes were used to cut down trees, to finish planks, and to butcher pigs; axes were used only for splitting logs. The same blades were used in both, and often a blade which had been hafted as an axe would be next hafted as an adze. Most of the blades in the Grand Valley are made of a fairly hard metamorphic epidote and clorite rock.

I was always impressed by the speed with which a Dani man could fell a tree with a stone adze, and I hoped to get good time studies which could later be compared with similar data on steel axes. As it turned out, a simple measure of elapsed time (I could not make more complex energy studies) was not very significant, since my subjects would hardly ever work straight through at a task, but would stop in the middle to talk with a friend, smoke a cigarette, and stretch before continuing. I have the impression, however, that the Dani may have increased the number of new houses which they built as steel axes came in. Certainly, they were not so careful to salvage all the lumber from old houses.

Using a stone adze to fell a tree.

Pig Tusks

Large pig tusks are often saved during the butchering and cut down and sharpened with flint chips. Some are used as tools, making fine concave scrapers to smooth down adze handles or spears; or they can be used as ornaments inserted through a man's pierced nasal septum and worn in battle.

Weapons

In fighting the Dani use both bows and arrows and spears. The bows are rarely more than 1.5 meters long, strung with a centimeter-wide bamboo band. The arrows are also short, measuring up to about 1.7 meters. They have a hardwood tip set into a reed shaft which is neither notched nor fletched. The weakness of the bow, together with the absence of stabilizing feathers, means that arrows are neither very accurate nor do they have a great range. I once went out with Um'ue to a level field where we tested his range. His longest shots fell between 90 and 100 meters.

The arrows are not actually poisoned but they are certainly dirtied. The hardwood tips are usually notched or barbed so as to break off and stick in the wound, and the very end is often wrapped with greased orchid fiber. If such a tip does break off and remain inside the wound, it can cause severe infection and eventually be fatal. They also have special two- or three-pronged arrows for hunting birds.

Arrows are used mainly for crippling people. The real killing weapon is the spear. Dani make their spears with great care from fine 3-meter lengths of myrtle or laurel which they buy from the Jalémo. A man will spend days straightening and smoothing and polishing and waxing his spear. It is much too valuable to be thrown, but it is a deadly jabbing weapon at close quarters.

Attire

Dani attire is mainly ornamental. It is not necessary for protection against the weather because the days are warm and the nights are spent usually indoors anyway. At a minimum, attire does serve to protect a person's modesty: By the age of four or so, a girl will begin to wear a little hanging skirt and a boy will wear a penis gourd. Two sorts of status are reflected in attire: males and females wear different things, and at marriage a girl changes her hanging skirt for a woman's braided cord skirt. The most important variations in attire within sex and age groups, however, are the result of individual preference. Some men like to wear more ornaments than others. Although there are more and less important men in Dani society, the fact is known to all, so it does not need to be communicated through attire. A stranger looking only at attire could not tell which of a group of men is the most important and which the least.

Much attire serves to protect a person's vulnerable spots from attack by ghosts. The ghosts can enter the body especially through the anus or the base of the throat, and most adult Dani wear something—a string, a band made of matted cobweb, or a leaf—hanging over these spots.

The Penis Gourd   From the age of four or five, males wear a *holim* or penis gourd at all times except when urinating or having sexual intercourse. These dried and hollowed gourds of varying lengths and sizes fit over the penis, are anchored at the base by a string around the scrotum, and are held upright by another string under the arms.

When I first began to study Dani artifacts, I was sure that the penis gourd would be a gold mine of data. Every man wore one. The gourds varied in length from navel height to chin height; in shape they were straight, curled at the ends, or curved; some were plain, others festooned with furry marsupial tails sticking out of the tips. In short, they promised to be a Freudian library of projective information giving immediate insight into basic personalities, rather like wearing one's Rorschachs on one's sleeves.

Alas, as data they were next to useless. People would have whole wardrobes of penis gourds of different lengths and shapes, and I could find no correlation between the gourd of the day and either long-term and short-term personality.

Even the general trait itself, which clearly seems to suggest a high Dani concern with phallic masculinity, is misleading. The Dani have little interest in sexuality (see p. 84), and the gourd itself is not a focus or symbol of masculinity or sexuality. We know of such exaggerated phallocrypts from cultures throughout New Guinea, from Africa, from South America, and from Europe (the braguetto, or cod piece of the fifteenth and sixteenth centuries) (see Heider 1969b). So the form is not unusual; the lack of significance is.

Thus the Dani penis gourd remains difficult to explain. The Dani have "always" worn it. It conceals (but does not protect) the penis, and people are never hindered by this apparently awkward thing. Boys soon learn to sleep in them, run in them, work in them, and even wage war in them. Through

A woman knits a carrying net in a cook house.

1970 at least, few Dani had any interest in exchanging them for cotton trousers. The penis gourd is a good example of a trait which persists because of cultural momentum. It has little meaning, but at the same time it does serve some functions and there are no good reasons to give it up. So it survives.

Carrying Nets   The women's carrying nets, in contrast, serve a multitude of obvious functions. In form they are large loose knitted string bags which hang down the back from a strap over the forehead. They are large enough to carry a baby, a piglet, or the day's harvest of sweet potatoes; they protect a woman's anus from wandering ghosts; and often a net decorated with dyed string or yellow or red orchid fibers is the only ornamentation which she wears.

Women make most of their own nets, although they are given special nets by their husbands at marriage and childbirth. The nets are knitted from string which is rolled out of fibers collected from wild plants in the forest.

ARTS AND PLAY

Art

There are countless ways to define "art," but according to most of them, the Dani have little or none. If art is (1) elaboration of something beyond the utilitarian, or (2) intended to communicate some aesthetic message to someone, then we have to look hard indeed to find examples of Dani art. Museums and private collections are proud of their pieces of "primitive art" or "tribal art," and many of the most striking pieces in these collections are masks, drums, and other sculpture from New Guinea. These days no one doubts their status as art, although the artists are usually anonymous, the cultures unknown, and their messages thoroughly filtered by distance and exoticism. In New Guinea it is the coastal and lowland cultures which produce the great art. The Papuans of the central highlands have little art, and the Dani even less than most.

Certainly, the men achieve craftsmanship when they spend hours working on a spear, heating and bending it to make it straight, and polishing it smooth. Then they color it so that two-thirds of the shaft is black, and the blade, red; these two parts are set off with a broad braided lime-whitened band. From a strictly utilitarian standpoint, the spear need only be a strong 3-meter-long pole light enough to wield in battle and sharp enough to kill. Clearly, there is nonutilitarian elaboration here, but it lies somewhat in that hazy area between art and craftsmanship.

The hafted stone axes and adzes often have interesting forms, but they are very utilitarian. Arrow points are usually elaborately notched and barbed, but here elaboration is lethally utilitarian. However, below the bars there are frequently engraved zig zags, dots, circles, and wavy lines. Carrying nets sometimes have added ornamentation. But few other artifacts have anything which even approaches art.

The most obvious visual elaborations are in personal ornamentation. Dani men have much personal ornamentation, more so than women, and they especially put it on for ceremonies other than funerals. During the hour or two before a ceremony or a battle, the men's houses are busy with activity as the men carefully prepare themselves. They pluck their beards; smear ash-darkened pig grease on their faces; set feathers in their hair; and fix all manner of head and body pieces which are decorated with feathers, furs, and shells.

The children have another graphic art form, a sort of graffiti, consisting of crude outline figures of people, animals, birds, and trees which they draw on rock overhangs in the forest. There are many of these rock shelters which provide convenient resting places for people working in the forest, gathering wood, vines, cigarette leaves, fibers, or whatever. Usually people make small fires to light their cigarettes, and the boys use the charcoal for their drawings. They are very ephemeral, soon fading away in sun and rain, perhaps to be replaced later by someone else. They are done most casually, and I am quite certain that they have no deep meaning.

But there are other designs which do have meaning. One day, after I had been with the Dani for two years, I was exploring some nearly inaccessible rock faces and came across a sort of cave area where the rock walls had many strange drawings, all done in red ochre. There were human hands in solid red; there were negative imprints of hands, made by placing a hand against the rock and then blowing powdered red stuff at them, so that the red formed the outline of the hand; and then there were birds, crescents, and some geometric designs. As much as I asked, no one was willing to tell me much about these drawings. My closest friends in the Wida moiety said that the figures had to do with the Waija moiety initiation. However, the Waija men disclaimed all knowledge, but they did seem amused that I had finally discovered the drawings.

In thinking about art crossculturally, we tend to concentrate on the visual arts and music. These are much more accessible to outsiders, since they can be appreciated without learning another language. The Dani certainly have much less visual art than most other New Guinea cultures, but it is less easy to make such judgments about their verbal art. By verbal art I mean that elaboration of language beyond purely instrumental communication. I never learned the Dani language well enough to really understand all its subtleties, but I was able to sense some of them. Koch, in the quotation cited on page 12, alludes to it. The Dani do not cultivate formal oratory, but some men are master storytellers. Dani conversations are a joy to watch, especially when a virtuoso brings all his verbal, paralinguistic, and nonverbal skills to the task. Now that synchronous sound equipment makes it possible, it would be good to have a film of this stunning, and surely artistic, Dani conversation.

They have songs also. There are the formal dirges of mourning and the songs of the victory dance, which have simple words or even just meaningless syllables. And there are the boys' songs, with a tremendous variety of verses set to a few simple tunes. Some of these are (in Dani terms) somewhat bawdy:

Dukhe, your husband has lots of fleas;
Niaige, your husband has lots of anal hair.

Others subtly evoke scenes in the landscape:

The reeds at Jibiga,
The reeds are twisted and turned;
The reeds at Belaloba,
The reeds are twisted and turned.

Alan Lomax, who has carried out worldwide crosscultural research on songs, has recognized song features which are characteristic of hunters and gatherers, and others which are characteristic of simple horticultural societies. The Dani of course are horticultural, but according to Lomax, their song style is that of hunters and gatherers (see Lomax 1962 and Heider 1967a). This remarkable finding strengthens the idea that perhaps the Dani are now still in transition from hunting and gathering to horticulture (see p. 34).

Curiously, although the Dani sing at ceremonies, at play, and when alone, there are no work songs. I think that only once did I ever hear anyone singing in the sweet potato gardens. This fits with the previous observation (see p. 48) that even when many men are working together, they are each doing similar things and not really coordinating in a task which has to be synchronized by song. The closest thing to a work song comes when a man is working hard; then he will often go into heavy exaggerated panting and puffing, almost making a joke of his labors.

Play

Trying to define play gets us into some of the same difficulties as trying to define art. Both are very familiar concepts, but good definitions are hard to come by. Play, like art, is nonutilitarian. But unlike art, it is done more for self-amusement than for aesthetic statement.

The Dani children play a lot. One might expect this of a culture with so much free time, where younger people are not drawn into full-time work. But what is most interesting about Dani play is that it is quite casual and unorganized. Children run about in groups, sometimes just exploring, sometimes having mock battles with grass stems as spears, sometimes making model houses. If we follow the classic definition of games (see Roberts, Arth, and Bush 1959:597) as organized play with rules, in which there is competition resulting in a winner, then the Dani have no games, for none of

Boys learn the skills of war in a mock battle fought with sticks in a fallow garden.

Dani play fits these criteria. In fact, the Dani seem to be one of the few cultures in the world which do lack games. Here again we find that the Dani are an exception to a general principle of human cultures.

But if we think of structure and competition as the main features which separate games from the rest of play, the Dani are less surprising. The Dani qualities of casualness and unstructuredness appear again and again in these pages. We have already noted the lack of intense competition and the absence of great social differentiation resulting from competition. Thus, the absence of games is consistent with other aspects of Dani culture.

Accident has provided us with a sort of experiment which reveals more about this pattern of Dani culture. At some time between my 1968 and 1970 visits to the Dani, the Indonesian schoolteachers introduced a game to the Dani schoolchildren in the Gutelu area. The fate of that game is interesting.

The game, Flip-the-Stick, is played widely in South and East Asia, and a variation is known in South Carolina and other parts of the Southeastern United States, where it is called "Roll-a-Bat." The Dani version has a batter, armed with a reed bat, who hits a short reed stick into the outfield, where someone else tries to catch it and throw it back to the goal (see Heider 1977). When it was taught to the Dani, it came as a real game, with structured rules and a way to count up the score and determine the winner.

What happened? In saying that Dani culture encourage nongame-like play, I am saying nothing about individual Dani's capability to learn games, only that they are likely to be disinclined to take up games. They are also culturally disinclined to learn the quantifications of arithmetic, but when that is taught in school and enforced by punishments for mistakes, they do learn it, more or less. But this game was introduced casually, at recess time, and the teachers did not try to keep it intact.

The result: The Dani children quickly perverted the game. They stripped it of its structure, its competition, and its scoring. In a word, they changed it from game to play. The most remarkable aspect of this process is that it was done by the children themselves, who were certainly not aware of all the implications of the conflicting cultural patterns. But it is vivid testimony to the strength of the Dani pattern that it manifests itself even in children.

I suspect that the schools will win out sooner or later. They have the power of all Indonesia behind them. And, of course, every day that a Dani child spends in school is a day away from Dani life. The years of youth, which once a Dani spent learning to be Dani, are now spent in school, learning to be Indonesian.

3 / Social Relationships

One way to find out about Dani social relationships is to sit in a compound, as I did, day after day, watching people come and go and interact. Slowly, one recognizes individuals, learns their names, works out whom they cook for and eat with and live with, and who comes to a funeral, bringing what, and who marries whom, and who gives what to whom at weddings. A pattern emerges, which begins to take on added dimension of meaning as one asks a Dani why someone did something, and he responds in terms of a real but invisible social structure of moieties and sibs and ties of blood and marriage.

There are two basic organizational sets which influence Dani life: the descent system, composed of patrilineal exogamous nonterritorial sibs and moieties; and the political system composed of territorial alliances and confederations. These two sets are crosscutting so that at any time any Dani is located socially in both sets. One effect of this crosscutting is that his fellows in one set are different from his fellows in another. That is, the members of a single sib live scattered in many different confederations, while the people who live together in one confederation are members of many different sibs.

TERRITORIAL ORGANIZATION

The Confederation

The largest persisting territorial unit is what I call the "confederation." (Alliances are larger, but as we shall see, they do not last long.) The Dani have no term for "confederation," although each confederation is named for the sibs of its most important men. The confederation which I know best is called Wilihiman–Walalua, a name compounded from the four sib names Wilil, Himan, Walilo, and Alua. Although confederations are long-lived, their membership is not permanent. People can move from one territory to another, finding friends and taking up land in their new locations. In fact, although we can call the confederation a territorial group, the social group is more important than a particular piece of land, and confederations stay

67

intact even if they have to move. This happened to the Wilihiman–Walalua after the massacre of 1966 when they made a shift to the south, vacating territory to make a no-man's-land on the north, and settling into the former no-man's-land on the south.

The confederation has flexible territory and membership. Furthermore, it is not a corporate group owning anything, and very little happens which involves the entire confederation. However, it does have a few formal functions. Certainly, the confederation is a meaningful unit to the Dani. They often use confederation names to describe people's homes or to locate events. We can call it a geographical unit because most confederations live on clearly bounded land, and it does have leaders, usually a couple of men who are generally recognized as the Big Men of that confederation. Perhaps the most important feature of the confederation is that, because it is a manageable size, everyone knows everyone else, and the conflicts which do arise within it can usually be resolved peacefully. To anticipate the later discussion of conflict (see p. 114), we can point out that this size factor means the confederation is the largest stable, peaceful unit, not usually split by war or feuds.

There may be 50 confederations in the Grand Valley. The Wilihiman–Walalua is one of the larger, with about 1000 people living on about 6 square kilometers, but some Grand Valley confederations have only a few hundred people.

The Alliance

The various confederations join together into larger units which I call "alliances." The Dani do not have a term for "alliance," and usually refer to a particular one by the name of its most important man. Thus, "Gutelu's," or "where Gutelu is." There are about a dozen alliances in the Grand Valley, each with several thousand people. Alliances occupy clearly bounded territories which are usually separated from the territories of other alliances by a no-man's land even in peacetime.

The alliance is the largest Dani social unit. It has two main functions: Wars are fought on an alliance basis between alliances, not within them; and the great Pig Feast is celebrated every five years or so simultaneously by the entire alliance. The most important Big Man of the alliance has ultimate ritual responsibility for a war and for directing the Pig Feast.

Although there is really no Dani social or political unit larger than the alliance, sometimes two or more alliances find themselves at war with a common enemy, but even then they do not undertake concerted actions. All 50,000 Grand Valley Dani have some cultural unity, with a common language and culture marked off from that of neighboring peoples; however, there is no social, political, or ritual unity to the Grand Valley. There are no events which involve the entire Valley population, and there are no leaders who are recognized throughout the Valley.

The Neighborhood

The Dani do not have a specific concept of what I call the "Neighborhood." But when we set up camp at Homuak and I began to get to know the nearest compounds, it became clear that there were people living in adjacent compounds who constituted an informal group in an unnamed behavioral setting. The 350 people in the two dozen compounds around the Dugum Hill had their gardens together and interacted more with each other than they did with the others in their own confederation. A population of 350 people was also a convenient size for me to focus on. Even though the Dani did not recognize it with a special label, it is a behaviorally real unit.

Compound clusters and compounds are even smaller territorial units, but, as we have already seen, only the compound is a real social and political entity.

In actual behavioral terms, then, the most significant units are compound, neighborhood, and confederation; the compound cluster is at best a pseudovillage; and the alliance is important mainly for warfare and the Pig Feast.

DESCENT GROUPS

Moieties

There are two named exogamous patrilineal moieties, Wida and Waija. That is to say, each Dani in the entire Grand Valley is a member of the same moiety as his or her father and marries only people of the other moiety. The main function of the moiety system is to regulate marriage through this rule of exogamy. The rule seems never to be violated. Therefore, for any Dani, half the members of the opposite sex are automatically ruled out as potential marriage partners. Given other limiting factors such as age differences and already-married status, a young Dani about to marry has a fairly limited choice of mates.

Moiety systems, especially exogamous moieties, occur throughout the world, but not all Dani groups have them. In fact, some Dani and their neighbors, the Uhunduni, have the only moieties reported from the New Guinea highlands at all.

Even though the Dani moieties are patrilineal, they have a complicated twist in the process of reckoning descent. All children are born into the Wida moiety, regardless of their father's affiliation. But later, at a Pig Feast, before they are to be married, those boys whose fathers are Waija go through an initiation or induction which makes them Waija. (Girls whose fathers are Waija automatically become Waija without ceremony.) So there is a kind of delayed-action patrilineal principle at work. I can suggest no reasonable explanation for this arrangement. At one point in the initiation ceremony a mass of Wida men make a mock attack with spears and bows and arrows on the Waija men and their sons (the initiates). Does this suggest perhaps that once the Wida and Waija were different cultures which merged and preserved the memory only in the ritual? I have no idea, but if there are Dani legends about this, I never found them. On the other hand, maybe there is no "explanation" of this sort at all.

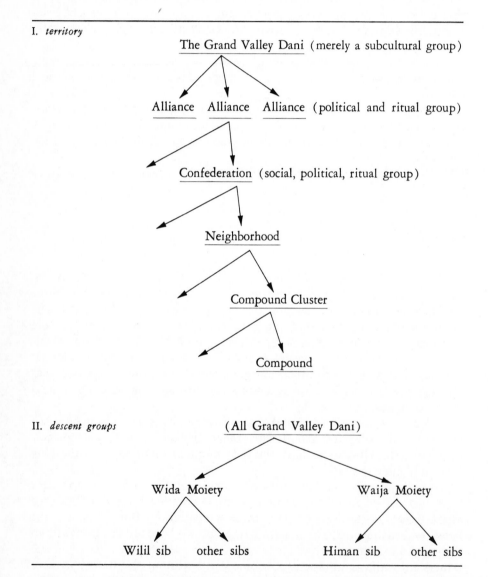

I. *territory*

The Grand Valley Dani (merely a subcultural group)

Alliance Alliance Alliance (political and ritual group)

Confederation (social, political, ritual group)

Neighborhood

Compound Cluster

Compound

II. *descent groups*

(All Grand Valley Dani)

Wida Moiety

Waija Moiety

Wilil sib   other sibs

Himan sib   other sibs

Diagram 4. The two principles of Dani organization: territorial political units and patrilineal descent groups.

Sibs

In addition to moiety membership, each Dani belongs to a patrilineal exogamous sib. People are born into their father's sib (and do not need to wait for an initiation of any sort). Each sib belongs to a particular moiety, so the rule of moiety exogamy automatically implies sib exogamy.

In the early 1960s I found people of 24 different sibs living in the Dugum Neighborhood, and over half of these people belonged to one of the five major sibs of the confederation. In all there must be about 50 sibs represented in the Grand Valley. Because there are similar or identical sib names among the Western Dani, this principle of organization may extend across the cultural boundary toward the west. However, the Gutelu people are so far from the Western Dani that I was not able to find out anything about this possibility.

Both sibs and moieties are nonterritorial, but with some differences. Any sib or moiety has members scattered across many confederations and alliance lines throughout the entire Grand Valley; but while in any one area this population is about evenly split between Wida and Waija moiety members, sib members are more likely to concentrate in some areas.

Sibs have several functions: (1) they regulate marriage, although this function is not very significant, since the sib exogamy rule is redundant with the moiety exogamy rule; (2) each sib is associated with a particular species of bird and sometimes also with a species of mammal, insect, or reptile; (3) sacred objects are held by sib members in common, and celebrated in ceremonies by the local men of a sib (see p. 128). (This ritual sib segment, then, is a convenient combination of territorial and descent groups.) However, members of a sib do not necessarily consider themselves descended from a common ancestor. They have common membership, not common descent.

BIG MEN AS LEADERS

Dani leaders are men of influence, not men of power. That is to say, leadership is a fairly informal attribute which does not confer power or the ability to force others to act against their inclinations. It also means that leadership must constantly be validated. There are no terms of office, and no way in which a person can suddenly acquire a tremendous increase in power by winning an election.

In a classic paper Marshall Sahlins (1963) distinguished two sorts of leaders in South Pacific island societies: the Big Man who achieved influence and the Chief who has inherited power. The Big Man is common throughout New Guinea and Melanesia and the Dani certainly share it. In fact, one word for leader in Dani, as in many languages, is literally "Big Man" (*ab goktek*).

But the Dani are even more egalitarian than most societies. Elsewhere the term "Big Man" really is a title for only the most important leaders; in the Grand Valley almost every man can be called *ab goktek.*

Hubugaijo, one of the few real gebu, *or men of no importance at all.*

At the opposite end of the scale of Dani leadership is the *gebu.* This term
has no easy translation. Its meaning is close to the term "Rubbish Man"
which is so common in eastern New Guinea, but like *ab goktek,* it is used
very loosely. A few men are indisputably *gebu,* but these are mentally defi-
cient, permanent bachelors who own little or nothing, and live as guests in
other people's compounds. The *gebu* whom I knew best spent about half his
time at Wubakainma, where he was genially tolerated. Sometimes he would
help the other men with their work, and once he made a small patch of
tobacco by himself. But mostly he would just be around, smiling inanely.

Gebu is a term which can be used in a disparaging way against any
man, both seriously and as a joke. When I tried these terms out on people,
they said they never used *ab goktek* for the few hopeless *gebu,* but even
Gutelu could be called *gebu* under the right circumstances. When I asked
for the names of the *ab goktek,* the lists would always begin with the most

*Um'ue, an important Big Man, stands in his courtyard outside a woman's
house, preparing to begin a ceremony.*

important leaders, never with the tallest or largest men. Yet there was some conscious use of the metaphor of height for importance: Someone of importance was described by the speaker holding his hands higher or lower above the ground, as if he were showing height. And sometimes people said that the brightest stars or planets were the heads of the really Big Men touching the sky.

Nearly everyone is to some extent, then, a Big Man in more than just a polite sense. Almost every man has some wealth, and can be a leader by

Mabel, the most important Big Man in the Alliance, directing the Pig Feast of 1970. At his throat he wears a great bailer shell ornament and under it a bib decorated with hundreds of nassa (snail) shells.

initiating some group action. Even a 20-year-old bachelor can call older men to help him with his garden. But one might make up a hierarchy or leadership roles which only increasingly important men can assume: Most men can organize a one- or two-day work task; fewer men can successfully host a funeral ceremony, keep the sacred stones of their sib segment, organize a watchtower group (that is, guard a border garden against enemy raids), or lead a raid themselves. Big Men with these capabilities are of the neighborhood or confederation level. The next step up, then, would be the one or two most important confederation-level Big Men who have responsibility for warfare on the local front, who perhaps have enough influence to keep the enemy trophies collected on their battlefields, and who run confederation-wide ceremonies. At the very top are the one or two most important Big Men of the alliance, who have ultimate responsibility for war and for the Pig Feast.

These levels are stated much more concretely than the Dani themselves see them, and I want to emphasize how fluid they are in practice. Over nine years I watched Um'ue move from being a second-level man in a confederation to becoming the Big Man of an entire alliance. In 1961 his Confederation, the Wilihiman–Walalua, was solidly within Gutelu's Alliance. But within months of our arrival, the older leaders of the Confederation moved to increase their own influence and independence from Gutelu by withholding the enemy trophies taken in a battle on their front. (The trophies are called "dead men" or "dead birds," and fortuitously, Robert Gardner in his film *Dead Birds* was able to capture the pivotal moment when Weteklue gave the order to take the trophies to his own compound. It was only much later that we realized how important that act was in the political development of the area.) This event marked the beginning of the rise of the Wilihiman–Walalua men, and within a few years, as Weteklue grew older and less active, Um'ue moved into the leadership of the Confederation. Then when Gutelu's people attacked the Wilihiman–Walalua in the massacre of 1966, Um'ue was in position to form a new and powerful alliance with Obagatok, a Big Man on his southern border. (The story is a long and complex one of gross manipulation and treachery on both sides.)

Men achieve importance by success in many fields. If one asks the Dani how to become a Big Man, they always say first, by killing many enemies and second, by having lots of wives and pigs. I was always suspicious of the completeness of this analysis, but it was hard to check out. I had little confidence that I had gotten an accurate figure on who had killed how many enemy. Perhaps in each death everyone involved got credit. In any case, straight-out killings may be less important than being clever enough to carry off a successful raid. In a battle, brave but relatively unimportant men like Wejak were often very visible on the front lines; men like Um'ue seemed to prefer action in the thickets off to the side.

In any case, aggressiveness and violence are not especially highly valued by the Dani. There is a category of men called *sinuknuk*. These are men who have acted too violently or too rashly in warfare or within their own group.

Sinuknuk implies something like "sometimes a little crazy," and people are wary of such men.

Another attribute, highly prized in anyone but especially characteristic of Big Men, is cleverness: *hat hotiak* is said to people in praise for some act that was particularly clever. *Hotiak* refers to the greatest Dani virtue, which is a cleverness, or an extreme competence.

Important men run ceremonies and have more to do with the sacred, or *wusa,* than do less important men. However, it does not seem that a man becomes important because he has special sacred power. Certainly, that was not mentioned by the Dani as an attribute of the Big Man. There were two exceptions: Gutelu, the leader of the Alliance, was said to have a special relationship with the *wusa* of the brine pool near his compounds; and Maikmo, leader of a small confederation, was supposed to have a special tie to the sun and the moon and could control rain. But these two men were exceptions. Generally, ceremonies are run by the most important men in an almost secular fashion. It would certainly not be accurate to talk about a Dani priesthood. Some men and women are supposed to be especially effective in curing people, and they are called on to arrange curing ceremonies which are as much to cure the individual medically as to drive away the ghosts which caused the complaint. But these talents are not institutionalized, and it might even be stretching things to call them shamans.

What seems to characterize the important men more than anything else is their skill in manipulating the exchange system; in other words, the degree to which they have established ties with many others through the exchanges. For example, another man in Um'ue's compound was Egali. He was very much of a loner, and not nearly as important as Um'ue. He had more pigs in his sty than did Um'ue, but they were always the same pigs. While Um'ue was continually giving and receiving pigs and shell goods at funerals, Egali held on to his. So although Egali at any one moment had more pigs on hand, Um'ue was worth more, in a social and economic sense.

Wealth per se does not bring influence, but a large household, several wives, and lots of pigs and shell goods, all go together as marks of the clever competence of the leader.

Leadership is not really inherited, but a boy who grows up around important men learns early the skills of leadership. Nearly all political and ritual transactions are semipublic, held in the common men's house, with boys casually present. Also, the sons of a leader take on some of his economic position. For example, we shall see that the marriage exchange continues for the generation after the wedding when the brother of a woman assumes his father's role in giving and receiving gifts. Because a Big Man is likely to have more wives than usual, his sons are likely to have more sisters and so be involved with more inherited exchanges than are most sons. In short, while it would be misleading to say that Dani leadership is inherited, it is certainly true that leaders tend to be sons of leaders.

Dani women do not have the same leadership roles as men. Young girls often go around with their fathers at ceremonies and can be part of a group discussing ritual or political matters. But when a girl nears puberty, she is completely excluded from such things. Only years later, as an older woman, can she rejoin these discussions. There is no Dani term like "Big Woman," and "Big Man" is used only for males. Women do have influence, but they rarely make important decisions or initiate activity. The influence which they have comes through their men—their husbands, sons, or fathers—and so it is dependent on both their own character and that of their men. Many Dani women are very independent and are more likely to act on their own, on the outside, rather than move into the inner core of decision making in the society. Thus, while women have no overt social or political power, they are personally not powerless, at the mercy of the men. Women do organize trips to the brine pool, and a few women are known as healers. These women, called by the special term *he phaphale,* sometimes organize and direct a small curing ceremony for a sick or wounded person. But for the most part, women are very much in the background. It would be very good to have more information on just how they play their roles in that background, however. It is pretty clear what women do not do, but one of the weaknesses of this entire ethnography is the lack of solid data about what women actually do.

KINSHIP TERMS

On the surface, the subject of kinship terms is a straight-forward one. Kinship terms are those words used to designate people according to their blood or marriage relationship to a particular person (the speaker, or Ego). Every society has a set of kinship terms. These sets are usually fairly elaborate and ideal for crosscultural comparisons because however complex and varied they are, they are all based on the biological fact that a man and a woman join to produce a child.

But when one deals with kinship terms, one has to make choices about how much data on each term to include in an analysis. For example, the English term "uncle" could be defined simply as "Ego's parent's brother," but there are many other "uncles." Even if one arbitrarily limits the analysis to relatives, one finds that uncles can also be "aunt's husbands" or older male cousins. Beyond actual kinship limits, nonrelated males who are close friends of parents are sometimes called "uncles." Then beyond that there are even more distant uses of the term: Uncle Sam, Uncle Tom, Dutch Uncle, and so on.

If one limits the description to the core meaning of each term, one loses much real information about how terms are actually used; but if one expands the scope of investigation, one has a mass of unruly data which cannot easily be compared with data from other cultures.

At the beginning I worked on just the core meanings in order to produce an elegant formal version of the Dani kinship term system. During my last trip, I was more interested in the total use of these terms. Here let us look at just a few features from both sorts of analyses (for a more complete account, see Heider, 1978).

Formal Analysis

Diagram 5 shows the most common Dani terms as used by a male speaker. If one studies this diagram, one sees that the system distinguishes people along the lines of age and sex. But within Ego's own generation there are more terms for siblings and parallel cousins, and several of these

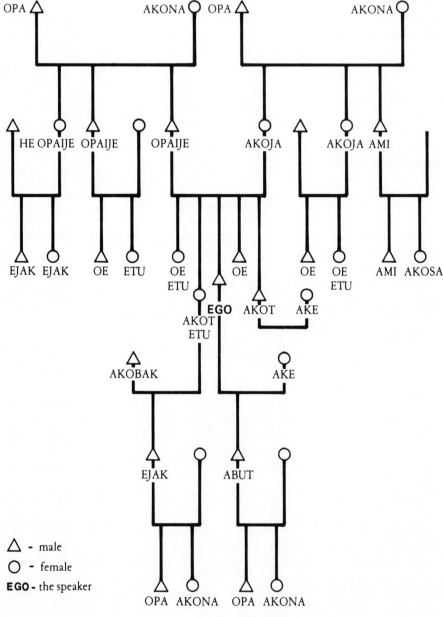

Diagram 5.   Dani kinship terms, male speaker (Ego).

distinguish Ego's older sibling (*oe*) from Ego's younger sibling (*akot*). The system is also consistent with the patrilineal moiety system. One can describe the rules for many kinship terms by using the moiety principle. For example:

> Men of the next generation older than Ego are called either *opaije* (if they are in Ego's moiety) or *ami* (if they are in the moiety opposite Ego's).

or:

> People in the first descending generation from Ego are called *abut* (if they are in Ego's moiety) or *ejak* (if they are in the moiety opposite Ego's).

This second rule is shown in Diagram 6, where terms for both male and female Egos are shown. In English we split that younger generation along lines of sex and laterality, thus getting "son" vs. "daughter" and "nephew" vs. "niece," or, using the useful new word *nibling* (like sibling, but for nephew or niece), we split just along laterality lines to get child vs. nibling. Dani, however, ignore both sex and laterality here, but they do attend to the criterion of moiety relative to Ego.

Dani kinship terms are used both as terms of address and as terms of reference. However, Dani more usually use another person's given name in addressing them if it is about a routine topic. In situations where they are invoking the particular kinship role, they are likely to use the appropriate kinship term. Thus, a younger man, in talking with Um'ue, might say, "Hey, Um'ue, look at this!" and then follow it a moment later with: "Hey, *opaije*, give me some tobacco."

A slightly more formal use of these terms reflects the fact that in many sorts of exchanges or gift presentations, especially at funerals, people of the same moiety are supposed to bring pigs, and people of the opposite moiety

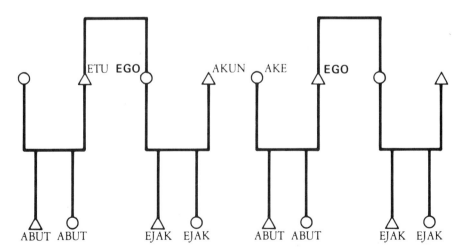

Diagram 6.   Kinship terms for first descending generation for both female and male speakers.

are supposed to bring shell goods. Thus, the proper way to acknowledge a gift of shells is to use the kinship term *ami* (one-generation elder male, opposite moiety): "*Nami wa! Nami wa!*" ("My *ami,* thank you! My *ami,* thank you!")

Although no one ever really tried to fit me into their kinship term system, when I would present someone with a shell, the usual response would be "*nami wa!*"

Although one might expect such important and fundamental words to be especially stable, there seems to be more dialect variation in kinship terms up and down the Grand Valley than in most other lexical areas. The terminology was also confusing to me at first because the Dugum Neighborhood is in a transitional area. Not only would two people use different versions of terms, but sometimes the same person might use both versions, for example, both *opaije* and *opase,* or both *akoja* and *akosa.*

Behavioral Analysis

The kinship terms in Diagram 5 are presented in traditional anthropological form, representing some basic features of the system, but the diagram actually tells us very little about how the Dani use kinship terms. It is a sort of map of the Dani realm of kinship terms, but if one were to walk into a Dani cook house with the diagram in hand, one would very quickly feel the need to know much more in order to understand how the Dani use these terms.

In 1970 I was more interested in the behavioral use of these terms, and so I asked about 100 Dani for all the terms which they used for all their relatives, and also for all the people for whom they used each term. The results looked very different from the map in Diagram 5.

The shape of Dani kinship-term space turns out to be very irregular. Many people use the terms in apparent violation of the formal rules. (These are, of course, the rules which I worked out, not the Dani rules.) Dani especially violate generation lines and moiety rules. They rarely use a term for the "wrong" sex, but I was surprised that they do seem to use terms for people of the "wrong" moiety. For a few positions, like father, there is general agreement that only one term (here, *opaije*) is appropriate. But there is much disagreement on other positions. (For example, several possible terms exist for older brother.)

I was especially interested in a matter of some theoretical concern: Are Dani terms used for categories like "older males, same generation" within which one person (here, father) may be the most important person; or are terms used primarily for a certain position (like father) and then by extension or analogy used for other similar positions (father's brothers, and so on)?

Again, the Dani system is irregular. When I asked, "Who is your *opaije?*" they all gave me the name of their own father first; yet when I asked, "Who is your *ami?*" more than half the people gave as their first (and presumably most salient) name someone who was not even related, and less than half named their mother's brother. These responses suggest that *opaije* is a category strongly focalized on father, while *ami* is a very dispersed category, focalized only weakly on mother's brother.

These sorts of irregularities do not show up in the standard kinship diagram. But until we have more comparative data from other cultures, I would hesitate to claim that the Dani are exceptional in their irregularity.

Learning the System

It may be that some of that irregularity is not inherent in the Dani kinship-term system, but is the result of errors. However, it is exceptionally hard to discover a set of firm rules for such a necessarily boundless system as kinship terms. There is only one statement I can confidently make about the Dani system in terms of an absolute principle: The moieties and sibs are patrilineal as well as exogamous. All adults agreed on that, and I found no evidence of any deviation from these norms. Thus, I used the understanding of these rules as a criterion of competency and made the assumption that if anyone was competent by this measure, then I would have to take their testimony about kinship terms seriously.

But many Dani are not competent. They do not understand their own system, and they make errors when talking about it. These people are, of course, the younger children, who were mentally quite normal, but had just not achieved full understanding. I did one study to discover the steps through which the children go in order to learn their own system (see Heider 1976a). By 1970, when I was asking these questions, I had only months, not years to get an answer. So instead of observing a few children as they were growing up, I talked to more than 150 children at different ages, almost 100 of whom turned out to be noncompetent. They were old enough to know some things about sibs and moieties and their own genealogies, but not far enough along to avoid errors. The most common sorts of errors which they made were claiming that their parents were of the same sib or moiety, or that they were of the same sib or moiety as their mothers, and different from their fathers.

By arranging these noncompetent children in order, one can get a probable sequence for how they learn about moiety and sib exogamy and patrilineality. The most common route seems to be to learn the principles of sib exogamy first, then sib patrilineality, then moiety patrilineality, and finally moiety exogamy.

Based on these results, it seems likely that for the children at least, sib membership is more important than moiety membership, for they learn to handle sib principles before moiety principles. Indeed except for marriage and initiation, both of which take place only during the Pig Feast, there is more activity on the sib level than the moiety level, and people are identified in terms of sibs first, moieties second.

THE FAMILY

Most Dani families are submerged in the life of the compound where they live with several other families. Very occasionally a Dani family lives by itself in its own compound. I knew of only one such example in the Dugum Neighborhood. A man, his wife and daughter, and his father lived alone. Only a few months after we arrived, the father died, making them the only residential nuclear family.

But normally, the nuclear family shares a compound with a wide range of possible others. It is hopeless even to try to generalize about the composition of a compound's population. One can find unrelated nuclear families, polygynous families, families extended vertically into three or even four generations or laterally with siblings and cousins, as well as the odd singleton unrelated to anyone. In some compounds all the men are of the same sib, even if they do not recognize actual blood ties; in others they are of different sibs and even moieties. At first glance a compound with one or two dozen people in it appears to be a randomly collected mob. The men are in the men's house most of the time, and the women and children cluster around the hearths of the common cook house. But family patterns soon emerge. A man goes into the cook house to sit at the hearth of his wife; she will cook for him; and he eats with her in the cook house, or with the other men in the men's house.

Although men usually sleep together in the men's house, they do sometimes visit their wives in the woman's house, and may sleep there. Public relations between husband and wife are usually pleasant and comfortable, but never demonstratively affectionate. I do not think that I ever saw a couple touch each other except accidentally or in the course of some task.

Polygyny is widely practiced. In the Dugum Neighborhood just under half the married men had more than one wife (see Table 3.1).

But these figures represent marriages, not household composition. Among the polygynous marriages some are actually coresidential, polygynous households, but in many the wives insist on quite separate residences in different compounds. Um'ue, for example, had three wives during most of

TABLE 3.1   DUGUM NEIGHBORHOOD MALES. MARITAL STATUS, 1963

Status		N
Not yet married		53
Never married (permanent bachelors)		3
One wife		49
More than one wife		43
2 wives	23	
3 wives	14	
4 wives	5	
9 wives	1	
	Total	148

(from Heider 1970:72)

the time I knew him. Two of the women liked each other, but a third always had uneasy relations with the elder of the other two. Finally, when the elder wife had a baby, and Um'ue's attention became focused on her, the third wife stayed more and more in her father's compound. She never actually severed relations with Um'ue, but for a period of some years she did not really function as a wife in economic, social, or sexual senses.

The polygynous marriage has many costs, but it does mean that every adult Dani can be married. In some societies, polygyny is maintained only at the cost of having large numbers of permanent bachelors or, at least, men who must wait until middle age when they can marry widows. The Dani system works out so that many more women are in the marriage pool than men. Two factors contribute to this: Women marry about five years before men, resulting in an extra five-year pool of eligible females; and the pool of eligible males is reduced by war deaths, which rarely affect the female pool. Thus, no woman beyond her late teens and no man beyond his early twenties need be unmarried. The only permanent bachelors and spinsters are a few seriously crippled or feebleminded men and women.

But it seems likely that these two factors which keep male and female marriage pools so unbalanced, war and differential age of marriage, will soon change. There have been few war deaths since 1966 (although this could change easily), and boys might become interested in earlier marriages. (On the other hand, if the young Dani men should begin to leave for a few years' cash labor on the coast, and then return as rich 30-year-old bachelors seeking wives, the situation would become immensely more complicated.) But take the simplest (and most likely) case: that pacification, by ending war deaths, balances out the marriage pools for men and women. Would polygyny continue at the cost of having unhappy bachelors? Or would the principle of monogamy for all prevail over retention of polygyny for the few? My first answer would be to predict that young men would find their wives and that polygyny would decline. This development would occur mainly because Dani society is too egalitarian and, perhaps, humanitarian for polygyny to continue at great social cost. However, this is one of those "all other things being held equal" answers. It is quite possible that for its own administrative convenience the Indonesian government will significantly concentrate power in the hands of a few Dani men who would then be in a position to ensure their own polygyny. We should begin to know the answer soon. (See page 163 of Chapter 5 for the outcome.) But certainly the institution of polygyny exists at the intersection of several forces which are changing and, in change, must change the institution.

Marriage Choices

The principle of moiety exogamy, which prohibits a Dani from marrying half the opposite sex, reduces the eligible pool even beyond the common pancultural restrictions which say that the other person must be approximately the same age (or the man be older) and that at least one should be unmarried.

If the Dani had moiety exogamy in combination with the sparse population of a hunting and gathering group, then a young person might be hard-pressed indeed even to locate a suitable mate. But the Dani have a population density of about 175 people per square kilometer, and since there is ample opportunity for movement within the boundaries of the Alliance, every person has several thousand people living in easy visiting distance.

The principle of moiety (and sib) exogamy is strictly obeyed. I heard of no marriages which violated it, and only one brief affair which did. On the other hand, there is no territorial exogamy, and people often marry close neighbors. In fact in a couple of cases I noted young men who moved into a compound containing an eligible girl in order to gain advantage in their courtship. In theory, cross-cousin marriage would be permitted, but I found no actual case of it in all my genealogies. Likewise, sororal polygyny is possible, but it is very rare.

The way in which marriage partners are chosen varies tremendously. When Um'ue and Obagatok united their confederations into a new alliance in 1966, they married each other's daughters. This was a political act worthy of the Holy Roman Empire, but perhaps not so successful. One of the young wives complained bitterly to me about the arrangement, and it seems unlikely that she contributed to a tranquil household. Other matches, though, are very much love matches arranged by the principals, even against the wishes of their families.

Postmarital Residence

Most marriages are between people from the same area, and the couple continues to live in that confederation. There is no dramatic clear-cut tendency for patri-, matri-, or neolocal residence. However, at the time of the wedding the bride is taken ceremonially to the groom's compound, which is usually that of his father. But within a few years, the married couple is likely to live in a compound apart from either set of parents.

Marriage and Sexuality

Although many marriages may be characterized by warmth and affection, there seems to be little concern for sexuality in marriage. In fact, the Grand Valley Dani have extraordinarily little interest in sex (see Heider 1976b).

A key to this low sexuality is the fact that the Dani have a postpartum sexual abstinence period of about five years. That is, for about five years—actually between four and six years—after the birth of a child, the parents do not have sexual intercourse with each other. Now this is quite an extraordinary claim. All cultures have some postpartum sexual abstinence, but it is usually only a few weeks or months long. Two years is a very long time. Five years seems quite unlikely. In many cultures there are special sorts of people who, by choice or circumstance, remain celibate for many years. Religious ascetics and widows are common examples. But all Grand Valley Dani observe this period of abstinence.

When I first reported the postpartum abstinence, I was met with two main reactions: The facts must be wrong; or if they are true, the Dani must have other outlets for sexuality during the five years. I am as certain as I can be about the facts, although one can never be totally certain about this sort of negative statement. Certainly the Dani men with whom I talked claimed that they observe the postpartum sexual abstinence, and although they had no way to say "five years," they indicated it by showing a child about that age as representing the length of the abstinence. In my genealogies I came across no full siblings born closer together than about five years. And there is no evidence for contraception, abortion, or infanticide which might provide such a genealogical pattern. In short, if we cannot impeach the testimony, we had best accept it and try to make sense of it. But "making sense of it" means understanding it in the context of Dani culture.

The problem is that a five-year postpartum sexual abstinence seems unlikely because of certain assumptions which we make about human nature. Derived from Freudian thinking, these assumptions hold that all people have a high level of sexual drive, or libido, which must either be expressed directly as sexual activity or, if blocked, must be rechanneled and expressed in some other ways. Late twentieth-century United States culture has so thoroughly absorbed this hydraulic theory of sexuality that even people who in no way consider themselves Freudians believe in it. Thus, on hearing that Dani couples practice a five-year postpartum sexual abstinence, the Freudians almost automatically begin to search for other sexual outlets hidden in the Dani data. (Interestingly, the people least surprised by the Dani turn out to be psychiatrists and psychoanalysts.)

Not only do the Dani observe the five-year postpartum sexual abstinence, but they have few other outlets for sexuality during that time. The one exception lies in the circumstances that because nearly half of the men do have more than one wife, during a postpartum abstinence they can still have sex with another wife. However, in those few instances which I could follow closely, the husband spent his time with the wife who had just had a baby, and ignored his other wives.

Although the men and boys of a compound usually do sleep together in the loft of the men's house, there is no sign at all of homosexual relations, and in fact I have no evidence of any other likely outlet for sexuality. Extramarital as well as premarital sexual activity is extremely rare. The evidence of this is fairly convincing: Dani life is quite public, and there are few places where one can be unobserved for long by adults or children. Only twice in my first two years in the Dugum Neighborhood was an illicit affair discovered, and each time there was great public commotion about it. It seems more likely that such affairs are rare, and less likely that they are common but successfully concealed.

Not only is there little sexual activity within or outside marriage, there is little concern for enforcing these norms. One can fantasize what would happen if somehow all this sexual restraint were to be made law in the United States today. The laws would have to be so harsh and so discordant with the culture as a whole that they would be very noticeable. The social control apparatus would have to be overwhelming: rigid segregation of the sexes, sexual police, closed-circuit television everywhere, and constant trials and punishments for offenders. The social and psychological costs would be enormous. But with the Dani there is nothing approaching this. When I pressed the question, people said that the postpartum sexual abstinence is enforced by the ghosts; if it is violated, the ghosts will cause trouble. But no one is much concerned, and I could find no overt signs of stress. This lack of stress seemed so significant that in 1970 I devised a videotape projective test to investigate it (see Heider ms.). Although in all my observations I found no sign of sexual stress, for the purpose of the experiment I assumed the opposite, namely, that men who were deep into their postpartum celibacy would feel differently about sex than men who had sexual access to their wives. The procedure of the experiment was simple: As each man sat before a videotape camera, I fed him a series of questions—some of which had to do with sex, others of which were neutral—and I recorded his answers. Then 20 people in the United States, who knew something about nonverbal behavior but did not know the Dani, viewed the tapes. The judges were not able to distinguish celibate from noncelibate Dani with very much accuracy. It would have been a great triumph for the videotape technique if it could have revealed things which were inaccessible to my ordinary ethnographic investigations. But in fact, by revealing so little difference among subjects, the experiment suggested confirmation of the ethnography.

I should emphasize that all my data came from the Dani men, and I do not know what the Dani women think about sexuality.

The Dani are clearly not asexual, however. They do have sexual intercourse enough to reproduce biologically. However, few women have more than one or two children. Table 3.2 is a simple breakdown of children per woman. These figures are on the low side, for it is likely that they do not include all conceptions or even births. They are at best accurate for living children. The table also does not give direct data on total expected children.

TABLE 3.2   NUMBER OF CHILDREN PER WOMAN IN THE DUGUM
NEIGHBORHOOD, 1963

Married Women Having Borne	N	
No children	13	(all young married women who have not yet begun to bear children)
1 child	86	
2 children	57	
3 children	13	(includes two women with twins)
4 children	1	(a woman with two children by each of two husbands)

(from Heider 1970:73)

One cannot tell how many more children can be expected from the childless females and from the women with only one child (most will have a second child). We have no way of knowing whether this is a long-time stable situation with the Dani, or perhaps whether we happened to catch them in a period of declining population.

There are no easy explanations for the length of the postpartum sexual abstinence. The Dani certainly do not live in a marginal environment where widely spaced births would have important survival value. Nutrition seems quite adequate, and infants never nurse much beyond their first year or at most two.

The postpartum sexual abstinence is only a part of the general pattern of Dani sexuality, and even if we cannot find a cause, we can at least note that it is consistent with the generally low level of sexuality. By this I mean specifically that there is neither a great deal of sexual concern nor much sexual activity. Even the penis gourd reflects this pattern. As described above, this apparently most phallic of male objects, which seemed at first to be a focus of great sexuality, is, for the Dani, a quite neutral covering.

Physical Punishment

Other aspects of Dani interpersonal relationships are consistent with the low sexuality. The general ambiance of a Dani household is calm and gentle. Both men and women like children, and people pay much attention to them, playing with them, talking with them, and touching and handling them. Children are almost never punished, even for what seemed to me like quite blatant misbehavior. I often watched a mother's reaction as her infant defecated or urinated in her lap or work area. Even if the child were a toddler, the mother would gently lift it away, clean up the mess, and continue with whatever she had been doing. In the film *Dani Sweet Potatoes* (Heider 1975a) there is a scene where a small boy takes a burning stick from a fire and waving it around approaches the dried thatch roof of a house. A man passes by, looks at the child, and moves on without comment. American audiences, sensitive to the dangers of playing with fire, gasp. But the boy is not punished, and he does not set the house afire. In another scene in the same film, a mother is harvesting sweet potatoes and her two-year-old daughter is getting more and more in the way. The mother happens to be a particularly short-tempered woman, but even under this provocation she does not take direct action. She "accidentally" hits the child with her elbow and then gently lifts it aside.

Even the ghosts share this gentleness toward children. In nearby forests there are some areas which have been marked off with taboo signs, warning that if a person intrudes to drink water or urinate, the ghosts will cause harm. But since they cannot understand the signs, children (and pigs) are not hurt by ghosts if they trespass. "The ghosts feel sorry for little children," one man told me.

Probably one of the greatest shocks to the Dani in recent years has been the physical beatings administered to adults by police and military, and to children by schoolteachers. Beatings for misdeeds were known to the Dani, although they were rare. But now beatings are meted out for ignorance and mistakes as well. When we discuss warfare, it will be evident that the Dani are no strangers to violence. But within the group and especially within the household, violence is extremely unusual.

Emotional Life

For the most part, Dani do not go to emotional extremes. They maintain a relaxed tone with each other. There is certainly affection, but rarely grand passion; annoyance but rarely an angry explosion. They must surely be considered gregarious, for people are rarely alone and there is little privacy anywhere. But for all their gregariousness, Dani do not seem to get deeply involved with each other. These impressions are the result of countless hours of just sitting around watching people, but in an attempt to get some hard data on this subject we did carry out some experiments.

Paul Ekman, a psychologist interested in facial expressions of emotions, was trying to establish whether or not some basic facial expressions were pancultural. We ran his tests with Dani subjects and found that, indeed, they had no trouble recognizing happiness, sadness, anger, fear, disgust, and surprise expressions. (The results are described in Ekman 1972:272.)

But as noted previously, Dani rarely get angry at each other. Two people are more likely to separate than to remain in confrontation and build up anger. Thus, on the replication of the Ekman test, the one mistake which Dani made with any frequency was to confuse anger with disgust. This tendency seemed like confirmation of the ethnographic observation: The Dani have a cultural norm for such situations (what Ekman calls a display rule): When they do get angry, they mask it with a disgust face.

I did one further experiment, asking some 23 Grand Valley Dani and 15 Western Dani to act out appropriate faces for different situations. The Western Dani, who live beyond the Grand Valley, are in many ways similar to the Grand Valley Dani; but they are much more volatile, and show extremes of emotions more readily. Thus, they provided a good comparison group. I recorded the facial expressions which they produced on videotape and later had Americans analyze them. The results were as expected. Comparing just "anger" and "disgust" faces from the two cultures, it turned out that both groups made good disgust faces, but that the Grand Valley Dani tended to make disgust faces even for anger situations. The Western Dani made fine anger faces and in fact even had many anger elements in their disgust faces. This sort of experiment is not by itself definitive. I do not recommend that it be substituted for hours of ethnographic observation. However, taken with the observational data, the experimental results help to strengthen the picture of the Dani as a people who have not only a low interest in sexuality, but a generally relaxed, nonintensive emotional range.

At the same time they are not a dull, lethargic people. They are energetic and alert, and the compounds often ring with conversation and laughter.

The Structural Positions of the Sexes

In nearly all Dani activities, men are found in groups at the center of things, and women are isolated on the periphery. The cooking hearths give a good example of this: Men sit around the central hearth of the men's house, facing each other, while in the common cook house, where the line of hearths runs along the central axis, each woman sits at her own hearth,

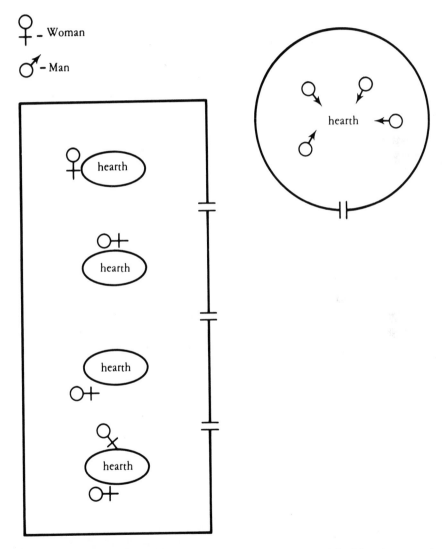

Diagram 7.   The structural positions of the sexes, exemplified by the men sitting around the men's house hearth and women at their hearths in the common cook house.

facing the entrances. Men's conversation is easy and face-to-face; the women's talk in the cook house goes in spurts, shouted over shoulders to some hearth farther down the line (see Diagram 7).

In large funerals there is also a clear spatial demarcation. Men sit toward the men's house, where the corpse is prepared and where the funeral goods are distributed; women sit at the other end of the courtyard, toward the entrance.

Women do participate in ceremonies, but it is usually because the man of their household does. Most women, however, are very independent in the sense of being able to run their own lives and to leave their husbands at will, and they are certainly not powerless in the face of their husband's commands. The division of labor is such that a man would be hard put to survive comfortably without a woman in his household. Yet, the other side of this independence is that women are also peripheral and unimportant in the social, political, and ritual activities of the group.

The schools may change this situation. Until the mid-1960s, Dani boys and girls had quite different lives. Girls spent most of their time with their mothers helping with chores, caring for the infants in the compound, herding pigs, and such. Rarely was there an opportunity for girls to spend time together. Boys led freer lives. They sometimes helped with the family pigs, and may have joined their fathers in big jobs like house building. But for the most part, boys were free to play, and one often saw gangs of boys wandering around the Neighborhood doing things together. Thus, for the crucial years of, say, 5 to 15, while the boys were learning social skills, the girls were doing routine tasks alone with their mothers. But since the mid-1960s, the government has made a concerted effort to keep all Dani children in school from about 6 or 8 to about 12 or 15 years of age. School not only keeps the children away from Dani things, it teaches them new patterns of behavior. One of these occurs on the playground at recess where, for the first time, masses of girls get together to play, interact, and practice being together in groups. The traditional Dani pattern certainly encouraged male bonding and female aloneness; the school system encourages female as well as male sociability. It seems likely that when these schoolchildren become adults this experience will change the structural positions of the sexes, making them much more similar.

SOCIAL CONTROL AND SOCIAL CONFLICT

Dani conflict is influenced by two quite different facts of life. The temperament of most Dani is quite peaceful and nonviolent, thus lessening the chances of real conflict. On the other hand, Dani institutions of conflict resolution are not particularly strong, so when serious conflict does occur, it is difficult to resolve.

Dani and "Law"

There is a running debate in the literature over the definition of law. It is immensely complicated by societies like the Dani. Strict interpretations of the concept of law would say that the Dani do not have law since they have no formal explicit legal code enforced by the agents of the society through the regular application of force. But this restriction is not a very useful one, and it does not help us to understand the Dani if we dismiss them as "having no law." They do not have statutes, judges, courts, or policemen, yet they are not anarchic or lawless. We need to talk about the Dani norms and how they work and what happens when they are violated. In addition, since violations of norms often lead to conflict, or are part of a conflict spiral, we need to talk about conflict and its resolution.

Dani norms are rarely made explicit. Of course, since they had no written language, they had no written code of laws. Nor do they have their culture summarized in a neat set of precepts, verbal formulae, or the like. The very implicit nature of the norms of Dani culture was most frustrating to me as a stranger trying to learn everything quickly. I am used to a culture where virtually all knowledge is codified in books and where many people can readily give instructions and explanations—where indeed the years of school are exercises in generating and handling these bits of knowledge. As a university professor I spend my time writing articles and books and talking formally about all manner of topics. Just one comparable teacher among the Dani would have made my task much easier. But the Dani are not accustomed to thinking about their own culture and explaining it, even to themselves. Dani children learn by watching and overhearing, not through direct verbalized instruction. I watched dozens of Dani houses being built, and almost always there were boys around taking part in the work. Although they were never given any sort of house-building instructions other than the occasional "take this" or "hand me that," by the time Dani youth are in their late teens, they are fully competent house builders. And so it is with all Dani knowledge. This absorption of casually presented knowledge is not as efficient as school and libraries; but Dani have much less to know than most Americans do, even though one Dani—or at least a Dani man and a woman—command most of the Dani knowledge and skills.

One can formulate explicit versions of Dani norms by watching what Dani do. For example, all Dani men's houses which I saw had round floor plans, and I never saw a Dani build a square men's house. A reasonable normative statement then is that "Dani men's houses have round floor plans." This is a technological norm, and not very interesting in a description of social control. In any case, I cannot explain *why* Dani men's houses are round—except to say, as the Dani do, "that is the way they always make men's houses."

Other norms which regulate significant interpersonal behavior are usually followed by the Dani in the same way, but when someone does violate them, it brings a powerful reaction from someone else. Here is where we find Dani legal behavior. After having insisted that the Dani do have law, I must admit that there is not much law and what there is I could not observe very closely. Let us look at an example:

Two young boys of the Neighborhood stole a pig from a Neighborhood man and took it up to the hills where they killed it, cooked it, and ate it. Everything was discovered almost immediately: The pig was missed and the little feast was spotted. The important men of the Neighborhood assembled at the most important men's house, and the fathers of the boys agreed to pay restitution of two pigs to the owner. The whole affair ran its course in an afternoon. This was a rare case, and I only heard about it after it was over. It made little stir.

Such moments, when the norms of the society are violated and reaction takes place to correct the situation, are, in many societies, arenas for dramatizing the basic principles of the society. They are public performances which serve to work out the guilt or innocence of specific people and also to explain and comment on the society itself. The courtroom drama is not only a staple subject in Western literature, but courtrooms, or courtplaces, are favorite sites for ethnographers to learn important things about a culture. Unfortunately, Dani judicial proceedings are brief, informal, and rare. In fact, I never saw one. But they seem to be effective within a neighborhood or at the confederation level when relatively minor groups arise.

Another case involved many of the members of the Wilil sib in the Dugum Neighborhood. A young woman married to an older Wilil man was discovered in an affair with a younger but much more important man of the same sib. There was a brief confrontation. I was in the gardens that day, and when I heard the shouting, I ran to the site. There had been a brief fight and arrows had been exchanged between partisans of both men. But all this was between people who were friends and it happened just outside the entrance of Wubakainma. By the time I arrived it was all over, and a man who had been on one side was busy removing an arrow from a man who had been on the other side. The whole thing was quite inconclusive. The husband beat his wife, and life went on. But a few months later the couple was again discovered, apparently actually committing adultery. This time the fight was more serious. The supporters of the husband faced the friends of the young man across some garden ditches. Again, these were allies, men of the same sib, who all kept their sacred stones in the same men's house. But now they were armed and shooting arrows at each other. The fight ended abruptly when a partisan of the young man was fatally wounded. The funeral was tense and afterwards the friends of the young man moved away, just beyond the Neighborhood, where they built a new compound. But the old ties were never broken, and the sacred stones were not divided.

Unfortunately, I was away from the Neighborhood at the time, and was never able to find out if there was any sort of legal process involved in this case. People said that more pigs and shell goods than usual were brought to the funeral, but this seemed to be more in sympathy than as an act of restitution.

There were few incidents of this sort, and this case was the only adultery which came to light during my two years in the Dugum Neighborhood. There were few pig thefts also. In fact, in most cases missing pigs turned out to be lost, not stolen.

In one instance one of a man's pigs disappeared from his herd. It was finally discovered that the pig had been rooting under a rock and had caused it to topple over, crushing the pig. But for three days previous to the discovery, the owner roamed the Confederation making increasingly tactless inquiries, for he was quite sure that someone had stolen his pig.

The judicial process is at best an informal conference among the Big Men which can recommend payment of restitution in case of theft, but has little way to enforce such a recommendation. The judicial process functions under the same constraints as were already discussed for the Big Man system of leadership: It must work through influence since there is no real power. This absence of power in Dani society is as characteristically Dani as the pervasive egalitarianism is.

Coping with Conflict: Withdrawal

The most common Dani way of coping with conflict is simple withdrawal. At a very early stage in conflict one party simply moves away from the situation. Individuals do it, and groups do it. The constant short moves of people within a Neighborhood and beyond are due largely to this avoidance pattern. When the move is made early enough, before unforgivable things have been spoken, the relationship can continue. When Um'ue's wife moved to another compound because of growing tension between her and his other wives, she could continue to drop in and help on important occasions. The group which moved out of the Neighborhood after a fatal brawl did so late, but still in time to prevent further bloodshed. Even children of eight or 10 can easily move in with a distant relative for a while, in hopes of avoiding the tasks which their parents were heaping on them.

In comparison with other societies, Dani interpersonal relations are less intensively focused on the family and more evenly diffused throughout the several hundred people of the Neighborhood or the 1000 people of the Confederation. By contrast, the American nuclear family living in its own apartment or house, forced by law (and economics at least) to stay together, is a real pressure cooker of emotions. No wonder that the U.S. homicide rate is comparatively high, and homicide within the family accounts for a significant portion of the total (20 to 50 percent according to different calculations). The Dani populations are so small that statistics are not at all comparable, but it does appear that murder (that is, homicide within an alliance) is very rare.

The pattern of withdrawal is intimately related to the lack of intense personal involvement, which has both benefit and cost. Withdrawal does reduce conflict, but it means that while not much conflict occurs within the family, not much of any other involvement occurs there either. It would be convenient to be able to propose a causal relationship but the case could equally well be made in either direction: Frequent withdrawal weakens the domestic ties, or weak domestic ties cause (or least permit) easy withdrawal. I do not think that we can answer the causal question here. Rather, we are building up the holistic context by showing the interrelationships between Dani traits.

CONFLICT

Serious conflict does arise between people for various reasons. Pig theft is probably the major cause. (Theft of other goods is surprisingly rare. I never ran across it.) Trouble between men over women does happen when adultery is discovered. Also sometimes when a woman withdraws from conflict in her husband's compound and moves in with a relative, the husband tries to get her to return and the conflict may shift to the men involved. Land disputes have occurred, although they are rare since most areas seem to have plenty of land available. The exception to this seems to be when two alliances are at peace, and people from each push into the no-man's-land between them to open new gardens. Then disputes over land do occur.

Dani conflict always begins from these or other causes between two individuals. If it is not resolved by some sort of mediation and restitution, or by withdrawal, it grows to include the entire territorial unit which is common to both men. In the fight over the adultery, all three principals were in the same sib. The fight briefly polarized the Neighborhood, but it did not draw in people from elsewhere in the Confederation. Such fights may be fatal but they are small-scale and brief, merely brawls.

But if conflict builds up between men of different confederations within the same alliances, it may break out into fighting between large groups from each confederation. Finally, if there is fighting between alliances, it eventually involves thousands of people on either side.

The Dani carefully distinguish between intra-alliance fighting, which they call *um'aim,* and the fighting between alliances, which they call *wim.* *Um'aim* is brief and purely secular. We can call it "feud." *Wim* may last half a generation, and involves the ghosts. We can call it "war."

Feud

Um'aim is rare, and although I never saw it, people did refer to it by name as an institutionalized form of fighting. Brawls within a confederation are "just fighting." The feud is more: it is *um'aim.* It still involves local people; it is not between enemies. The term *aguni juma-mege* is a friendly term, meaning "local people," "people from here." The people of another alliance are *dili,* or *aguni dilimege,* which means "the foreigners," "the aliens," the present or potential foes. This distinction is purely political, for dialect variations are likely to occur within an alliance, or conversely, enemy alliances are likely to share virtually identical cultures.

Also, as we shall see, the Dani believe that the ghosts of the slain demand revenge when the killing occurs across alliance boundaries in war. But in brawls or feuds, when people are killed by their own kin or neighbors, the ghosts do not demand revenge.

WAR

War was an immediate part of Dani life. Every Dani alliance was constantly at war with at least one of its neighboring alliances. Every individual Dani was touched by war. People who lived near a frontier, like those of the Dugum Neighborhood, could see and hear battles, and whenever they went to their sweet potato gardens, they had to be alert for enemy raids. Every Dani had seen friends and acquaintances dead or dying from spear wounds or arrows. Most men had helped to kill an enemy in that way, and everyone had often attended "fresh blood" funerals. In this section I shall describe the full traditional form of Grand Valley Dani warfare as it existed through my first five months of fieldwork. Since the early 1960s, government efforts at pacification have wrought many changes in Dani warfare, but before discussing these, we should deal with the older form of war.

When the Harvard–Peabody Expedition arrived in the Grand Valley in March 1961 and set up camp in the Dugum Neighborhood, we were immediately thrust into an ongoing war between the Gutelu Alliance (which included the people of the Dugum) and the Widaia (an alliance in the middle of the Grand Valley, on the left bank of the Balim River). For five months we watched it. We went to battles, we heard raids, and we attended funerals. Robert Gardner was able to shoot considerable movie footage of the fighting, which he later incorporated into his film *Dead Birds.* At first the warfare seemed a timeless thing, and we studied it for the moment. Only gradually did the shape of war emerge. Next to the battlegrounds in the no-man's-land between the Gutelu and the Widaia were old fallow gardens grown over with young trees, and a few groves of banana plants where once compounds had stood. It was clear that once there had been peace along that frontier, but it was years before I learned anything of the history of the fighting. The real clue to understanding Dani warfare was the realization that it occurs cyclically in two forms. A brief outburst of violence, the secular phase, sets the political stage for the years-long duration of the routine of the ritual phase of war. We saw only a few months of one ritual phase. The rest of this analysis is reconstruction. Perhaps someday someone will work out a complete political and military history of the Grand Valley alliances. Meanwhile, I can sketch part of it as seen from the corner where the people of the Gutelu Alliance live.

In the early 1960s the Gutelu Alliance was fighting against the Widaia and included confederations on either side of the Elogeta River. But several decades earlier, probably in the mid-1930s, the Elogeta had marked a no-man's-land between the Gutelu Alliance to the north and another alliance to the south, which then was made up of the Wilihiman–Walalua and the Widaia. This alignment was shattered sometime in the 1940s, when the Wilihiman–Walalua split from the Widaia and joined Gutelu in fighting against their old allies. The different versions of this shift emphasized different aspects of it. Some say that Gutelu simply talked to the Wilihiman–Walalua of the wisdom of joining him. Others say that it happened as an act of betrayal: One day, when the Wilihiman–Walalua were ready to move, they came to a battle ostensibly to fight with the Widaia against the Gutelu, but instead they turned against the Widaia, routed them, and joined with Gutelu. In that shift the Wilihiman–Walalua stayed on the bulk of their old lands. They did have to abandon fields and compounds bordering the Widaia along the Aikhe River which had become too vulnerable to raids. They were able to move up to the banks of the Elogeta into territory which had been no-man's land.

For the next 20 years things were fairly stable. Then in 1966 the Gutelu Alliance exploded as Gutelu's people made a surprise attack across the Elogeta on the Wilihiman–Walalua compounds. When the dust had settled, the alliance boundaries were back more or less to where they had been 20 years earlier: The Wilihiman–Walalua were again with the Widaia, and a no-man's land was opened again along the Elogeta River.

Toward the end of this history, the central government played a part, but not enough to obscure the Dani pattern. In the late 1950s the Dutch government of Netherlands New Guinea had established a post at Wamena, and from there they began to pacify the southern part of the Grand Valley. They did send a few patrols into the Gutelu area, killed a Dani in a skirmish, and imposed a short-lived peace. The Dani were impressed with Dutch firepower, and I heard several dramatic accounts of the damage which the bullets had done to the man killed. Apparently, the Dani felt that peace was permanent, for they moved into the no-man's-land, opening fallow gardens and even building compounds with Widaia. But the Dutch patrol did not return and the peace did not last. By the time we arrived in early 1961, the hopeful settlements were long abandoned and overgrown and that area was again a battlefront.

Government involvement was more definitive in September 1961 when the Dutch again sent in patrols, demanded an end to warfare, and established a police post in the Wilihiman–Walalua Confederation area to enforce it. This action marked the end of formal ritual battles, but even the Indonesians who succeeded the Dutch in 1963 were not able to stop the great massacre of 1966 which split the Gutelu Alliance. Some accounts suggested that the behavior of policemen and soldiers actually contributed to the conditions which lead up to the massacre. In any case, the government troops did take quick counteraction in 1966.

By the mid-1960s, then, the presence of outsiders was playing a role in Dani warfare. Although the focus of this section is on Dani warfare as it existed until September 1961 in the Gutelu area, the later events can also help us to understand what was going on.

The Ritual Phase of Warfare

For the five and a half months from early April to mid-September 1961, we were able to observe Dani warfare on the southern front of the Gutelu Alliance where they were engaged with the enemy Widaia. During this time there were nine battles (although two of them never really got going) and nine raids. Six men and boys were killed in the raids. No one was killed in the battles, but I knew of two men on the Gutelu side who died from wounds received in these battles. There was an average of one battle or raid a week on this southern frontier. But as the following chronology shows, action was quite sporadic, and sometimes a month would pass without a battle. As we shall see, the Dani say that war is necessary to placate the ghosts, but there is no exact correspondence between which side initiates a battle and which side has taken the latest loss. During the same time other Widaia and other Gutelu were similarly engaged on other parts of the frontier to the north, and men from the Dugum Neighborhood occasionally went to a distant battle.

A Chronology of War: An account of battles and raids on the southern frontier, April–September 1961

The southern frontier of the Gutelu Alliance lies in the Dugum Neighborhood of the Wilihiman–Walalua Confederation. The major battlefields are the Dogolik and the Watabaka (Map 5). The Gutelu in the following description are men of the Gutelu Alliance, but for the most part only men from the Wilihiman–Walalua, Gosi–Alua, and Wilil–Himan confederations of the Alliance are involved in the fighting on this front. The following events have also been described by Matthiessen (1962) and Gardner (1963). Broekhuijse's account (1967:232–78) is by far the most extensive, for he was able to make extensive and efficient use of informants during the crucial months of the battle. He described immediate details of battle and participants' opinions that could not be replicated after the events were long past.

10 April. Battle called by the Widaia; challenge accepted by Husuk, a young Gosi–Alua leader. Fought on the Watabaka. Fighting commenced early, about 8 A.M. By 9:30 wounded men being carried back. Fighting ended by rain, 4:30.

15 April. Battle called by the Gutelu. Fought on Dogolik. About noon, fighting was broken off by the appearance of a white man (one of the expedition party returning from Wamena). By two o'clock many men were leaving the field. A few stayed, shouting insults at the Widaia. By three o'clock the insults were too much to bear in silence, and the Gutelu streamed back onto the field. Fighting was resumed for another two hours until ended by dusk. (One Widaia died six weeks later from wounds.)

4 May. Battle called by the Gutelu but challenge was not taken up by Widaia. One group of Gutelu waited on the Watabaka, another along the Aikhe River. By noon, when no Widaia had appeared, they gave up and returned home.

11 May. Raid on Widaia gardens by Gosi–Alua under Husuk. One Widaia killed in his watchtower. After the kill, the Gosi–Alua massed on the Watabaka, were joined by other Gutelu, and waited for Widaia to appear for a normal battle. They didn't.

25 May. On a northern front the Gutelu killed an Asuk Balek, an ally of the Widaia. People of the southern front prepared for dance to celebrate death.

26 May. Battle initiated by early-morning Widaia raid up the Aikhe River. Gutelu quickly responded, and the Widaia withdrew to the Dogolik where they asked for battle. Gutelu refused, saying they had to dance for the man killed the previous day. Widaia made a second thrust up the Aikhe River. The Gutelu finally accepted the battle. Battle was to be fought on the Watabaka, which by this time the Widaia controlled in total. As the Gutelu moved into the swamp to approach the Watabaka, the Widaia withdrew from sight. The Gutelu, fearing an ambush, approached the hill carefully, finally massed at the base, and rushed the summit of the short arm of the L. They took it without opposition, finding the Widaia properly withdrawn to the long arm of the L without opposition. Sporadic fighting. By two o'clock both sides withdrawn a bit, sitting, shouting, taunting. Then half an hour of fighting around the bend of the L. Then disengagement, the Gutelu withdrawing to middle of short arm of L. As the Widaia moved away along the long arm of the L, the Gutelu, led by Husuk, began triumphal singing. Suddenly the Widaia turned and charged at full speed. The Gutelu held them for a time, and then, in unusually close and fierce fighting, the Gutelu dropped back and finally were pushed off the hill completely into the swamp and bushes. The Widaia stood on the crest of the last knoll, taunting in their turn. Finally they dropped back and both sides went home.

29 May. Widaia announced that a man has just died from wounds received on the Dogolik (battle of April 15). Dance begun but abruptly terminated about 1:30 when report of Widaia raid on northern frontier is shouted in.

4 June. Widaia sent in raiding party, set up ambush at edge of gardens. No one was caught, so at 5:30 they raided the then-deserted gardens and burned the Uwenebaka watchtower shelter. Then they withdrew to the Dogolik, where the Gutelu rushed, and fought for fifteen minutes before both sides went home at dusk.

5 June. Widaia massed on the Dogolik and called battle in early afternoon. Those Gutelu men within hearing responded immediately but were far outnumbered, so stopped at point on Dogolik where the strip is very narrow. Thus the front would be narrow and the numerical advantage of the Widaia could not be exploited. At the same time, a group of about fifty Gutelu faded into the swamp, prepared to attack the Widaia flank. The Widaia did not advance to meet the Gutelu, and the afternoon rain sent both sides running for home.

7 June. Morning raid by the Widaia, who burn a shelter, uproot potato vines, trample tobacco, and break a dam, letting water run out of a duck pond on the Dogolik. The Gutelu came to meet them on the Dogolik, and by eleven o'clock a battle had developed here.

8 June. Tracks of unsuccessful Widaia raid discovered. Apparently they had come up the Aikhe River and penetrated as far as the Anelatak, found no one, and returned home.

10 June. Widaia raid up the Aikhe River, kill Wejakhe, young boy. Wilil *ganekhe* ceremony had left the gardens and watchtowers deserted. Wejakhe, two other boys, and one man went to the river to drink, were surprised by Widaia ambush; Wejakhe was killed, others escaped.

22 June. Battle called by Widaia on Watabaka. Some Gutelu crept through the swamp and waited on the east slope of the Watabaka in hopes that the Widaia would walk over the crest into the ambush. Nothing happened. Finally the Gutelu broke the ambush and occupied the short arm of the L. Fighting began at the bend of the L. One hundred Gutelu crept into the woods on the inside of the L, and those in the open tried to draw the Widaia back into an ambush. This was also unsuccessful. Finally the ambush broke and the mass of the Gutelu rushed the Widaia. Shouting and cheering, the Gutelu pushed the Widaia back up the long arm of the L and finally off the hill together. By 5:00 the Gutelu stood on the hill, taunting the Widaia. There was no further engagement, and both sides finally went home.

5 July. Raid on the Widaia gardens, called by Weteklue. The raiding party was apparently spotted by Widaia lookouts; a counterambush was set up, and one Gutelu, Jenokma, was killed.

2 August. A Widaia pig turned up on the Gutelu side of the no-man's-land: perhaps strayed, perhaps stolen, perhaps a bit of both. The Gutelu, expecting retaliation, went to the Watabaka, and a battle developed on the flat ground between the Watabaka and the Siobaka hills. Desultory fighting, with relatively few men on either side. The high point of the day when a *jokoik,* the large cuckoo dove whose cry is the signal for battle, flew low over the Gutelu warriors. Everyone dropped his weapons and tried to hit the bird with all available missiles. It flew away but returned to be greeted by a large supply of sticks. It escaped uninjured.

6 August. Gutelu attempted raid on gardens beyond Watabaka. This failed, and battle developed on fields between Watabaka and Siobaka hills. Along the banks of the stream, a boys' front. Boys as young as six, standing on either side of the stream, shooting arrows at each other, coached by older man. About noon the skirmishing became desultory, and Nilik, in angry disgust with his men, called them back to the Watabaka Hill. By 3:00 the Widaia had occupied the field and were taunting the Gutelu. The Gutelu charged down the slope and fighting resumed. But once again Nilik was disgusted and called his men back. Then both sides withdrew to their hills—the Widaia to the Siobaka, the Gutelu on the Watabaka. For an hour or two they exchanged words rather than weapons: derogatory references to individual enemy's wives, to the stolen pig; a choice phrase would bring forth a peal of laughter from the comrades; a good blow from the other side would be met with jeers of derision. The Widaia, who had a wider repertoire of bird calls than the Gutelu, used trilling, jeering calls to good advantage. No one made any further attempt to fight. They sat in the setting sun, shouting. A good time was had by all.

16 August. Early morning raid by the Gutelu to the Widaia gardens near the Subula. One watchtower overturned. Battle developed on the strip, far beyond the Dogolik. Desultory fighting, with a two-hour rest in the early afternoon.

24 August. Widaia woman crossed the no-man's-land seeking refuge in Abulopak. Weteklue decided to kill her, but she was escorted out of the region by a member of the expedition.

25 August. Four Asuk Balek men, allied to the Widaia, visited Abulopak. Two have relatives there. The other two were attacked in the early evening. One escaped, the other was killed.

Early September. Widaia raid deep into Gutelu territory, killing one young boy. Gutelu raid into Widaia territory, killing two Widaia. The next day a government police post is established between Abulopak and Dagulobok, effectively pacifying the southern frontier. Warfare continues unabated on the northern frontier of the Gutelu territory.

(from Heider 1970:310–313)

Battles

Battles are formal events involving hundreds of men which take place for a few hours at midday on one of the battlefields in no-man's-land.

Each battle is sponsored by a Big Man in a confederation. He takes major responsibility for what will occur: He has a claim on any trophies which will be taken, but he will also have some of the blame if anyone is killed. There are several men in any confederation who can assume battle leadership. (In the Wilihiman–Walalua Confederation, one man, Weteklue, usually called battles.)

The evening before, a Big Man holds a ceremony for his men to prepare for the battle. This is called *elak gabelhatek,* the sharpening of the spears and arrows. It serves to put everything in readiness for the following day,

From the rear lines, resting warriors and noncombatants—old men and boys— watch the progress of the battle.

and especially to enlist the aid of the ghosts. A pig is killed and shared among the warriors, and then a portion of it is set aside for the ghosts. (I only found out about this ceremony in my later fieldwork, after pacification, so I suspect that there may have been important details which no one thought to mention.)

The sponsor of the battle sends a messenger toward the front to shout across a challenge to the enemy. Usually, the challenge is accepted by a comparable Big Man on the Widaia side, and a battlefield is agreed on.

Then the whole countryside erupts in the cry of the *jokoik,* the large cuckoo dove—literally a war whoop—as word is passed across the entire alliance. It is a clear message. Everyone knows where it originated, so they know that there will be fighting that day on that front. The cries are both announcement and invitation.

When the *jokoik* call passes up the Grand Valley, it is still early, misty, and cold. The men take advantage of the next hours to prepare themselves, while the sun burns away the night mist. Both men and weapons are smeared with cosmetic pig grease. Men arrange feathers in their hair or adjust their various ornaments. Everyone is attired differently, but all are elegant.

Depending on his personal preference, a man is armed with spears or bows and arrows. The spearmen carry long, finely crafted jabbing spears and often a couple of cruder short spears which they can throw at an enemy. Bowmen carry the short bow and a handful of arrows, barbed, notched, and often freshly dabbed with sooty grease to cause infection. Men also carry tobacco nets slung over their shoulders, holding cigarette makings for times of rest behind the front lines.

Young boys, some only eight or 10, hang around the edges and then go forward to the battlefield with the warriors from their compounds. The boys do not actually fight, but they are allowed to carry things for the men, and of course they watch the battle closely, learning how to be warriors.

Not every Dani man goes to battle. Some are always there, some never go. No leader has the power to force a man to participate, and there is not even any obvious social pressure: There is no disparagement of either occasional or regular noncombatants, no concept of cowardice in such cases. Once, as I was hurrying toward a battle with a group of men, we passed through a sweet potato garden where a man and his son were working. The men all exchanged a few words of greetings, but there was neither surprise nor accusation of shirking a duty.

But most men do attend. The main fighting is done by the younger men, from about 15 to about 25 or 30 years of age. Older men carry their weapons to the battle and may join in briefly. But after age 40 or 50 a man will stay in the rear lines, watching and shouting encouragement at the fighters.

By about 10 in the morning a couple of hundred men have arrived at the battlefield. The local men arrive in small groups from their various compounds. Sometimes a mass of warriors would arrive from elsewhere in the Alliance. They all usually assemble just out of sight behind the battlefield, and then make a sudden noisy colorful entrance.

There are two favorite battlefields on this southern frontier (see Map 5). One is the Watabaka, a 1.5-kilometer-long, low rocky ridge bent into an L shape. The Widaia would occupy one arm of the L, and the Gutelu the other; the battle would sweep back and forth among the rocks in plain view of all. The other site is the Dogolik, a long open grassy strip of high ground running through a swamp.

By noon the battle is under way, and it will continue in fits and starts for several hours, or until rain has driven the men to cover. At first a few men run toward the enemy, who are still far beyond arrow range. For a few minutes they shout taunts, whoop the *jokoik* cry, wave their weapons and

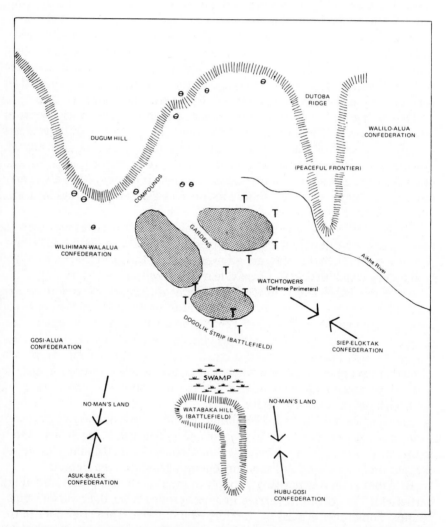

Map 5.   Southeastern war frontier of the Gutelu Alliance, 1961. (Heider 1970:115)

their feather whisks, and then retire. Some of the enemy reciprocate. Gradually, the lines get closer together and soon they are within firing range of each other.

The archers let off one arrow after another at the mass of the enemy, but since everyone is watching each arrow, there are rarely any hits. Arrows can be shot in a flat and reasonably accurate arc at 10 or 20 meters range, but anyone who is that close to an enemy is watching and dodging. As men dance up to the front, they can take care of themselves. As they drop back, though, they have a blind side and many wounds are received then.

Occasionally a man will shoot for distance, but these arrows take high wavering paths which can easily be seen by an enemy. Long shots do pay off when the lines have shifted enough to catch someone who had thought that he was safely in the rear and had dropped his guard.

Spearmen and archers work together, with the idea that the bowmen will bring someone down with an arrow so that he can be killed by a spear. Spearmen throw their short spears if they think that they have a good opportunity. Very occasionally I saw a man throw his fine long jabbing spear. This was usually a mistake, but he could sometimes manage to retrieve it.

Battle. (Photograph shot with 500-mm lens)

The front continually fluctuates, moving backwards and forwards as one side or the other mounts a charge. Its composition changes as men move up from the rear, stay to fight for a while, and then drop back for a rest. Those on the front, in the most vulnerable positions, must keep in constant movement to avoid presenting too easy a target.

Battles are exhilarating. There is danger, of course. Many men walk away with painful arrow wounds and some must be carried home to spend weeks recovering. But for most, a battle is full of excitement. There is a tremendous amount of shouting, whooping, and joking. Most men know the individuals on the other side, and the words which fly back and forth can be quite personal. One time, late in the afternoon, a battle had more or less run out of steam. No one was really interested in fighting anymore and some men began to head for home. Others sat around on rocks and took turns shouting taunts and insults back and forth across the lines, and connoisseurs on both sides would laugh heartily when a particularly witty line hit home. But as lighthearted as the atmosphere sometimes gets, battles are definitely not just a game, not merely a welcome change from the routine life of sweet potato farming and pig herding. They are fun, entertaining, and adventurous, but battles, and war in general, are a more important core of Dani life.

Action in battle is constrained in many ways. Of course, one characteristic of war in all cultures is that it is constrained in some way. Out-and-out mayhem is the exception. While some societies have explicit codes or laws of war, the Dani norms of fighting, like their other norms, are implicit.

For example, Dani never shot arrows in volleys. Their short, inaccurate arrows coming one at a time are easy to dodge. But if a dozen archers were all to shoot simultaneously at the same man, he would most likely be hit. I suppose whenever I was on a battlefield I had somewhere in the back of my mind an image of Laurence Olivier's movie *Henry V,* with its great scene of the Battle of Agincourt, where the English archers shot flight after flight of arrows in disciplined volleys. I always longed to ask a Dani why he did not shoot in a similar way, but I never did, out of fear that I might thus be responsible for a major escalation in the bloodiness of Dani warfare.

The Dani manner of shooting is consistent with the general individualism of movement on the field. There is very little in the way of formal maneuvering. A group of men from one area may move to the front in a block, but once there, each man acts more or less on his own. Often Big Men would stand on a hill to the rear, shouting warnings and directions. It was easy to imagine that they were something like battlefield commanders, directing their troops. But it soon became apparent that this interpretation comes from the images of our own culture. In fact these men were hardly commanding, and whenever they tried, no one was obeying.

Another sort of constraint, this one technological, is that no Dani arrows are fletched. Actually, no New Guinea Highland arrows are fletched so in one sense the Dani are not exceptional. Yet the Dani do make complicated ornaments with feathers. Why did they not feather their arrows? This apparently minor innovation, which was certainly within their technological capability, would dramatically increase the accuracy of their arrows. It is possible that here we have an invention on the brink of being made. It is also possible that the Dani in some sense do not want to make their warfare more efficient. There are other indications of this possibility. For example, everyone knew that we had a shotgun with which we killed ducks on the Aikhe River. People often watched us hunt and admired the results. Also everyone knew that guns could be used on people, for Dani had been killed by Dutch guns. Yet no one ever suggested using our gun in their battles or raids.

Now, I am not suggesting that Dani leaders once sat together in council and forbade fletched arrows, shooting in vollies, tight formations, or guns. Yet if the sole aim of war was killing enemy expeditiously, the Dani could not be considered very skillful. We need to consider war as having many functions, and killing is only one of them.

Removing an arrow.

In our five months of observing, we approached battles very cautiously. The first time one occurred we hardly knew what to expect. Michael Rockefeller and I sat on the Dugum Hill above camp, watching with binoculars, as Gardner, Broekhuijse, and Matthiessen moved slowly forward toward the battlefield. By the end of that day it was clear that we were free to do what we wanted. We were quite irrelevant to both sides. We were so far outside the Dani system that we were neither an embarrassment to our hosts nor were we targets for Widaia arrows. But we were perhaps too careless, and I still wonder that none of us was ever wounded. Once, at a battle on the Dogolik, I had moved off the high strip into the bush on the side to get a feel for the sort of skirmishing going on there. The Widaia had not seen me, and were shooting arrows at random, hoping to hit someone. One arrow landed a few meters in front of me, and a moment later another hit just behind me. I moved back to the open battlefield quickly.

In another battle, this time on the Watabaka ridge, Michael Rockefeller and I were standing among our friends photographing the Widaia. Suddenly, we realized that we were quite alone, our friends had left the ridge, and the Widaia were advancing. We moved off the ridge into the swamp and stood watching the Widaia occupy the entire ridge and our camera bags. We felt very exposed and foolish. But the Widaia thought it all a huge joke. They shouted, "Hey, come live with us, you don't want to stay with those people." Soon they withdrew and we sloshed out of the swamp and recovered our equipment, quite intact.

The expedition had a small motorboat, and every week or two we made the trip down the Aikhe River to pick up supplies and mail and send out exposed film from Wamena. But the Aikhe flowed directly through Widaia territory. At first we were somewhat apprehensive about seeming to consort with the enemy. The Dani themselves are wary of magic being sent from the enemy. Thus, the people of the Dugum Neighborhood do not eat ducks from the Aikhe River because they may carry a Widaia poison upstream. Once when they had recovered the body of a man killed during a raid into Widaia country, they carefully neutralized the various magical things which the Widaia had stuffed into wounds and orifices.

But it turned out that we were harmless, and no one was worried about us. The day after one battle I took the boat down the Aikhe, and at every Widaia compound people were waiting, drawn by the sound of the motor. They all wanted to know if a certain man, whom they knew had been wounded the day before, had died yet. I said no, not to my knowledge. When I returned to the Dugum Neighborhood, our friends were all curious about the trip, and asked the same question: Had I seen any signs of a funeral preparation among the Widaia? There was great disappointment when I again had to say no.

A good indication of Dani feelings came when, in August 1961, we took Um'ue in the boat to Wamena to see the government town there. In order to smuggle him past the Widaia, we dressed him in our clothes. On the way down he sat quietly as we passed the Widaia compounds. But coming back he took off his hat, sunglasses, and shirt, and shouted out greetings to the

Widaia on the banks. Finally, we had to stop the boat so that he could have a long conversation with some of the same men he had just faced on the battlefield. If he had come alone, he would certainly have been killed. But with us, he was out of context, and shared our neutrality.

Raids

There are two quite different forms of fighting in the ritual phase of warfare, namely, battles and raids. The battles are publicly announced engagements of hundreds of men in which there is much action but little bloodshed. The raids, on the other hand, are surprise attacks on enemy gardens by a few men who hope to kill, and often succeed.

Battles engage most of the men of the two opposed confederations in addition to their respective allies. A raiding party is more often made up of a dozen men from one neighborhood organized by a rising young leader. The men go into raids with no ornaments, moving unseen across the no-man's-land to the edge of enemy territory. They hope to find a careless person alone in a garden or someone coming to the river for a drink, or even to trap a man in a watchtower. But the no-man's-land is known intimately to both sides, and the defenders who are on the lookout for raids are quite familiar with all possible routes and ruses, so the raid is dangerous for the raiders as well. One raid made by the Gutelu men was discovered and trapped by the Widaia, who managed to kill a young man without losing any of their own people.

Although the goal of raids is death by surprise, even they are limited by implicit norms. No raids occurred at night, even during nights of the full moon. (This is another fact which I was unwilling to ask about too closely. I could imagine a reaction: "Hey! Gatoto asked why we didn't have raids at night, and that gave me a great idea. . . !") Ghosts are dangerous after dark, of course, but few people seem to take that seriously if they have something which they really want to do, and in any case, no one worries about ghosts when the full moon lights up the countryside. So I think there are no raids at night not because of fear of ghosts but because there are limits to Dani warfare.

The Lines of Defense   No defense is really necessary in battle, for both sides come knowingly to it. But raids are quite different matters. All border land is vulnerable to raids. This includes most of the Dugum Neighborhood. Many other neighborhoods, set farther back from the frontier, are totally immune from raids. There must be some selection of population here, for some people choose to live in danger and others choose safety.

The people of the Dugum Neighborhood have an ingenious mixture of technological and magical devices which protect them from Widaia raiding parties. The most conspicuous of these is a series of watchtowers which runs along the farther edge of the gardens, facing the enemy. Each tower is a column of poles bound together with heavy vines. On the top is a small platform from which a man can survey a sector of the no-man's-land. Some platforms are only 5 meters or so high, but others go up to ten meters. When the watchtower is built, a small symbolic bow is slipped into its base and steamed grass is laid in a circle around it in order to induce the ghosts to help guard the area. The men who have gardens in one area will build the watchtower together, and they have the responsibility for manning it. In the mornings, after the sun has burned through the haze, these men take up their weapons and go ahead to the gardens, scouting for enemy raiders. Then the women follow. Through most of the day one man stays up on the watchtower while the rest of the men lounge about in a small shelter near its base talking, smoking, weaving shell bands, working on their weapons, or just sleeping, and women work in the gardens. The watchtower shelter, like the men's house, is forbidden to women, but they often build little lean-tos in the gardens for shelter against rain. The watchtower system is extremely important in defense; thus, raiding parties which cross into enemy territory only to find the gardens empty, often tear down watchtowers or burn the shelters in frustration. The Dutch also recognized their importance, and when they finally pacified the Gutelu–Widaia frontier in 1961, they had all the watchtowers dismantled. But the Dani had less than complete faith in pacification since it had not lasted the previous time. They did not actually rebuild the watchtowers, but they avoided outright defiance of the Dutch by using convenient trees as lookout stations.

There are other defensive devices. The raiding parties have two routes across the no-man's-land. One is along the banks of the Aikhe River, and the other leads through swampy terrain. There are a few relatively firm paths through the swamp, but in wet weather especially, if one is not familiar with the way, it is easy to go off the track and become hopelessly bogged down (as I found out more than once). The usual Dani bridge over a ditch or stream is a simple log. In this swampy no-man's-land the people of the Dugum laid their log bridges under water, thus giving tremendous advantage to the home team. If one knows where these hidden bridges are, one can run through the swamp. If not, one flounders at the mercy of an enemy. But I assume that the Widaia gain the same advantage by laying submerged bridges on their side of the swamp.

There are two sorts of early warning systems beyond the watchtower line. One is a small shelter about half a meter high in the woods near the Aikhe River. It was built to attract ghosts—with the idea that if a Widaia raiding party should come by, the ghosts would shake the trees, and the waving treetops would warn men in the neighboring watchtowers.

The ducks on the Aikhe River are quite skittish, and take flight noisily if anyone passes along the river bank, so they, too, help defend the Aikhe border. The people of the Dugum Neighborhood do not eat ducks, ostensibly in order to avoid the Widaia magic. Another result of their abstinence was that the duck population was maintained at a high level. (At the time, we shot ducks for the expedition table with a double clear conscience. The Dani obviously did not want them and it gave us fresh meat without dipping into the limited Dani supply. But in retrospect, I am afraid that we were actually decimating their forward sentries.)

The Dani extended the effectiveness of their duck defense by digging a small pond at a strategic spot a few hundred meters away from the Aikhe River. The pond rarely went dry, and usually after the last people had left the gardens in the afternoon, some ducks would settle in for the night. The next morning they would make a loud departure when disturbed by the first passersby. No raiding party could have moved through that area without raising the duck alarm.

The Role of the Ghosts   Throughout this account of raids and battles, reference has been made to ghosts, for they play an important role in Dani warfare. The Dani believe that when people die their ghosts remain in the vicinity of their homes and are a potential cause of trouble for the survivors, but in warfare the ghosts can be induced to assist against the enemy. Ghosts along the frontier help to raise the alarm at the approach of an enemy raiding party, and they actually help kill enemy in battle. The ceremony which is held the night before a battle is apparently intended in part to send the ghosts over to the enemy side, where they select out a victim to be killed on the battlefield the next day. There is a feeling that human weapons need this ghostly assistance in order to kill an enemy.

In a more important sense, it is the Dani belief in ghosts which keeps warfare going. At the time, when I asked the Dani why they fought, they always said "because of the ghosts." If a man was killed by the enemy, his ghost would lurk around causing various sorts of misfortunes until the people managed to kill one of the enemy in return. Thus, the killing in war, once begun, developed its own internal energy. Of course, since the Gutelu and the Widaia had the same ghost beliefs, a killing which relieved one side of ghostly pressure only created it for the other side. However, there was not a strict one-for-one accounting of deaths. For instance, in August 1961, the Wilihiman–Walalua had lost two men to the Widaia, and they seemed to feel special pressure to kill at least one enemy. It is significant that this practice was not exactly a system of revenge killings, although it took more or less that form. Instead the people saw their main goal as placating their ghosts, not retaliating against the enemy.

The Ritual of War   It seems reasonable to call this long-term sequence of battles and raids "the ritual phase of war" partly to distinguish it from the other phase, in which ghosts do not figure, and also to emphasize the Dani understanding of their own warfare. It is not just the act of killing which is important to placate the ghosts; there is also the whole complex of expressive behavior which proclaims the efforts being made by the people on behalf of the ghosts. The Dani know how to kill an enemy: They stage a raid. If battles are meant to produce deaths, they would have to be counted in most instances as failures. Although no Dani ever put it to me quite in this way, it seems reasonable to say that the battles, with all their noise, action, and display, are ways to communicate with the ghosts.

The Edai *Dance of Victory*   The communication with the ghosts is most evident after one side has succeeded in killing an enemy. Then for two days they hold a ceremony called *edai*. On a special *edai* field in plain view

Women and girls dance at an edai *for an enemy death. In the left foreground stands a bundle of spears, arrows, and other items taken from the enemy; these trophies are called "dead men" or "dead birds."*

of the enemy, the entire confederation comes to dance and sing. The dance is simple: groups of people move back and forth, or around in circles, shouting, whooping the *jokoik* call, and singing. Men, women, and children join in, wearing as much finery as they can and carrying weapons. This sense of spectacle is heightened by the appearance of the women, for this is the only time when they wear shells, feathers, and furs and carry spears and bows and arrows. For two days they dance, sing, and display trophies taken from the enemy, weapons as well as ornaments. The noise probably reaches across to where the enemy are holding the funeral. When the Widaia had cause to *edai,* they came to the ridge of the Wakawaka battlefield, where they could be seen as well as heard from the Dugum Neighborhood. But the *edai* has a double significance. The people are aware that in killing an enemy they have placated their own ghost, but they also know that now the enemy has a fresh ghost of its own which demands placation with blood.

The Secular Phase of War

The cycle of Dani warfare is a years-long series of battles and raids between alliances of confederations, broken by a brief outburst of fighting which splits alliances and rearranges the constituent confederations into new alliances, setting the stage for a new series of battles and raids.

During the early 1960s the Gutelu Alliance had shown signs of internal stress. In particular, the Wilihiman–Walalua were discontent with Gutelu's leadership. In part this may have been because the Big Men who had maintained the alliances, like Gutelu himself and Weteklue of the Wilihiman–Walalua, were getting older, and young leaders like Um'ue of the Wilihiman–Walalua, Mabel of the Dlabi–Mabel, who lived near Gutelu, and Maikmo, whose Wilil–Himan were unfortunately placed between the

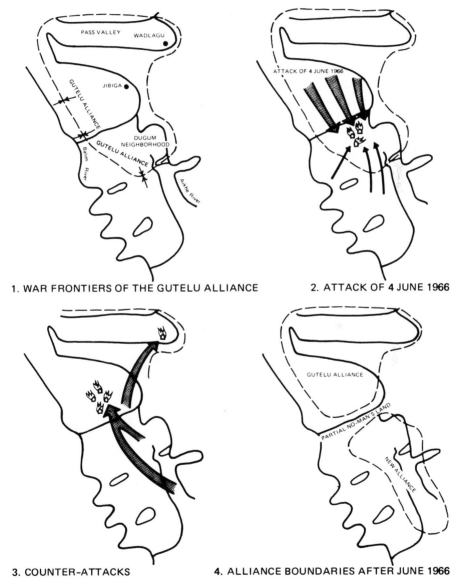

1. WAR FRONTIERS OF THE GUTELU ALLIANCE   2. ATTACK OF 4 JUNE 1966

3. COUNTER-ATTACKS   4. ALLIANCE BOUNDARIES AFTER JUNE 1966

Map 6. Frontiers before and after the attack of June 4, 1966. (Heider 1970:120)

two, were beginning to become respected leaders. The Wilihiman–Walalua made a few tentative moves in the early 1960s. In 1960 Weteklue began to keep the war trophies from the southern frontier instead of sending them north for Gutelu to hold. In 1963 Weteklue and the other Wilihiman–Walalua Big Men tried to start the Pig Feast on their own. This prerogative is normally reserved for the most important Big Man of an alliance—Gutelu—but they felt that Gutelu had delayed too long. For reasons I never learned, their attempt did not succeed, and in the end they celebrated the Pig Feast with everyone else in 1964. Meanwhile, over the years there had been an expectable number of minor conflicts over pigs, women, and other matters, which arose between people of different confederations. Probably, even in traditional Dani days each of these incidents would have been unresolved and would have gone toward building up strain within the alliance. But after 1961 there was a government post in the Wilihiman–Walalua area, and the police entered many of these cases on the side of their Wilihiman–Walalua neighbors, bringing their force to bear against other confederations in the Alliance. I am sure that without the police presence, the tension would have been building up anyway. Whether or not the police intensified it is arguable; they certainly did little to reduce it.

The break finally came in 1966. Before the mists rose on the morning of June 4, hundreds of men of the northern Gutelu made a surprise attack on the nearest compounds of the Wilihiman–Walalua. In an hour they had killed about 125 people and burned many of the compounds (see Map 6).

I heard details of this attack from missionaries as well as Dani when I returned to the Grand Valley in 1968. It was very different from the other acts of war which we had seen, especially in terms of its motivation: While the battles and raids were necessary to placate the ghosts, this had nothing to do with the ghosts. It was direct human revenge, retaliation for endless annoyances. It was a deliberate political act ending what had become an unsatisfactory alliance. It was also a move by Mabel to wrest leadership from Gutelu. Accounts differed to some extent, but credit for the attack was generally given to Mabel, a man of about 40, who belonged to a confederation closely associated with Gutelu's own, and who lived near Gutelu in the heart of the Alliance territory. Apparently, Gutelu had cautioned against such an extreme step. This warning reflected Gutelu's prudence, not mere timidity. He knew Indonesian power better than most Dani. He had been to the coast and had even been one of the "tribal chiefs" who were flown to Djakarta to meet President Sukarno. But Mabel went ahead with the plans. He enlisted all the leaders of the confederations to the north of the Elogeta River. This left only those south of the Elogeta: the Wilihiman–Walalua and their close associates, the Wilil–Himan and the Gosi–Alua. Mabel also went farther afield and invited other nearby alliances to join in. The night before, it is said that Mabel went to Gutelu, told him about the plans, and gained his powerful ritual support.

Mabel had timed the attack well. The police post was nearly deserted that day, and the priest at Jibiga, near Gutelu's home, was in Wamena for a visit.

The position of the Dugum Neighborhood at the very southern extreme of the Alliance had always put it in the greatest danger from the Widaia, but on this day the enemy were on the other flank of the Confederation and most of the Neighborhood was out of reach of the attackers. By all accounts the attack was well coordinated and effective. A dozen compound clusters were hit at once. The attackers put houses to the torch and then waited by the doors for the inhabitants to crawl out so that they could cut them down with spears and also with machetes, a weapon new to Dani warfare. The sties were opened and pigs freed. Apparently, all the actual fighting was done by Mabel's men. But men who had been invited in from other alliances made off with countless pigs. However, as far as I could learn, there were no instances of rape at all. Eventually, the attackers withdrew. The survivors were left with a devastation the likes of which a Dani might see only once in a lifetime. Ordinary funerals were out of the question. Um'ue and the others tore down fences for wood to build great funeral pyres on which they threw all the corpses.

By the next day word of the attack had reached Wamena, and Indonesian forces were on the scene. They marched through the northern Gutelua Alliance area, eagerly guided by the men of the Wilihiman–Walalua. Perhaps two dozen people were killed during this punitive raid-cum-counterattack, but most of the northern compounds were burned.

Within days peace had returned. The Elogeta River compounds were smouldering ruins, and that entire area was abandoned by both sides to become a no-man's-land. Obagatok, a Big Man of the Widaia, had stayed out of the original attack, but joined Um'ue in the counterattack. Thus was born the new alliance, led by the two new leaders.

The secular phase of war differs from the ritual phase in many respects: It is rare, it is short, it is very bloody; women and children, as well as men, are killed; property is destroyed and plundered; and it is done for motives of secular revenge.

Ending War

It may be that Dani wars do not end; they just move on. Over the years the Wilihiman–Walalua Confederation has always been at war with someone. Even as their alliances form and reform, the killing continues and there are always ghosts to be placated and enemy to be killed.

War Deaths

It is difficult to get good figures for war deaths. I was based in a frontier neighborhood, so the people were frequently engaged in warfare, and the war deaths among them were probably higher than the war deaths for the entire alliance. In addition, people would tend to remember war deaths more than ordinary deaths, thus further inflating the figure. But because my sample is small and I saw only five months of actual warfare in 1961, it would be foolish to claim that these figures are really representative of the entire Grand Valley. There are several ways to make an estimate. During the five months of warfare in 1961, four people were killed out of a population of about 2000 (the Wilihiman–Walalua and Gosi–Alua Confederations). This would give a rate for war deaths of .48 percent per year. (Myron Bromley once figured a rate of 1 percent per year in the southern Grand Valley [1962:23].) On the other hand, that same population of 2000 lost about 125 people, or 6.25 percent of the whole group, in the massacre of 1966. But this quite extraordinary event had never happened to them before.

Another way to figure war deaths is to look at genealogies. Here I found that 100 of 350 (or 28.5 percent) of deceased males and five of 201 deceased females (2.4 percent) were killed in warfare. But war deaths are especially memorable, and the "fresh blood" funerals are particularly important, so there is undoubtedly a tendency toward remembering war deaths.

Interpreting Dani Warfare

Dani warfare is the outcome of certain structural features of Dani society, and can be described in those terms. It is also an immediate bloody encounter between people, usually hand-to-hand and often fatal. So it also needs to be discussed in experiential, psychological terms. Because Dani warfare is an institution with broad ramifications throughout Dani life, it must be treated in a holistic sense.

Warfare as a Structural Outcome   Although it is misleading to try to isolate *the* cause of Dani warfare, the main precipitating factor of the secular phase of war is unresolved trouble cases between people of different confederations. These cases build up tension between the confederations and eventually war erupts. Although subsequently, it is the ghosts which keep the war going, it was those individual conflicts which started it off. Now it is worthwhile to turn to earlier discussions of conflict resolution, leadership, and power. There is little real power available to anyone in Dani society, and leaders are men of influence, not of command. The legal system works extremely informally through these influential men. For many reasons it is quite effective in resolving interpersonal conflicts at the local level where everyone is so intimately interrelated. But in some senses the confederation is the largest Dani social unit which is fully operational. Confederations do join in larger alliances for purposes of war and the Pig Feast. But the alliance is not only unstable, as we have seen; it is also too large to have an effective system of conflict resolution. Or, to put it the other way around, the Dani legal system has so little formal power that it is not effective beyond the confederation boundary. If two men within a single confederation get into a dispute over a pig, the Big Men of their confederation will be able to work things out. However, if men from different and even ostensibly allied confederations have trouble, they each will be supported by their own confederation mates, and there is no effective alliance-wide system to adjudicate matters. Even Gutelu was first of all a member of his own Dloko–Mabel Confederation before he was leader of the alliance.

The structure of Dani society also helps to understand why wars continue long after their original causes are forgotten. The war deaths themselves become grievances between opposed confederations, but there is an anomaly of structural levels: Although wars are on the alliance level, pitting all of one alliance against all of another, these grievances and unanswered killings are between opposed confederations. Thus the Big Men of the confederation can keep the war going, but no overall alliance high command can coordinate a peace for all its constituent confederations, each of whom, in a sense, is fighting its own war against those confederations of the enemy alliance which face it across the no-man's-land.

War and the Individual   There is an apparent paradox if one contrasts the picture of the individual Dani as gentle, nonaggressive people who withdraw from conflict with the picture of their warfare, which demands constant engagement and often homicide on the part of these same people. I have indicated this central paradox of Dani life in the subtitle of this study, calling them "peaceful warriors." The key to both domestic peace and external violence, however, seems to be their detachment or interpersonal noninvolvement. In a sense, both harmony and violence come down to casual indifference. In warfare there is no anger at the enemy, no indignation at his acts, no feeling of personal revenge. Perhaps we must say that these emotions appear only during the secular phase of war, and even then they do not last. I was quite astounded in 1970 to watch veterans of both sides of the 1966 massacre calmly comparing notes on these events, and in 1961 I was quite surprised that the Dani men took pacification by the Dutch with such little concern. I had expected a lot of redirected aggression to emerge in fights and perhaps suicides, but there seemed to be none. At least I anticipated that my closest friends would complain to me about the end of warfare since they had complained about everything else the Dutch were doing, but they did not.

A distinction must be made between violence and aggression, for it will help us to sort out Dani behavior. These two words have many meanings, and for some people they are nearly synonymous. But I would like to suggest here that violence is the use of force against another, while aggression, although usually violent, implies an inner state, an intention to overcome or dominate an enemy. Using the two terms in this way, we can say that killing a pig in a ceremony is certainly an act of violence, but it is not aggression. So although the Dani are violent in warfare, even in war they are not often aggressive in any useful sense of that word. People whose only knowledge of the Dani comes through seeing the film *Dead Birds* are often overwhelmed by the dramatic scenes of the violence of warfare, and they then jump to the conclusion that the Dani are a very aggressive people. The data presented in this book, however, show the violence of warfare in the total context of Dani life, a context which turns out to be quite nonaggressive.

A Holistic Summary of the Institution of War

We come back to the question, "Why do the Dani fight war?" The answer cannot be a simple one. It will be clear by now that the institution of Dani war is complexly embedded in Dani life. The attempt to find one strand which can be elevated to a prime cause is futile, but we can make a systematic summary of the place of warfare in Dani life along the lines already used for describing the Dani men's house.

In Diagram 8 the institution of warfare is shown in relation to conditions and effects. The conditions are precedent to warfare, and in some ways bear on the shape of the institution. The effects are outcomes of warfare. The whole diagram is simply a systematic summary of Dani warfare in context. The ritual and secular phases of war are treated differently to some extent, although they share many of the same conditions and effects. It is also important to distinguish between the Dani explanations and those other factors which emerge out of the ethnographic analysis.

Dani Explanations for the Ritual Phase   The Dani explain the ritual of warfare in terms of the ghosts: It is caused by the ghosts' demand for revenge, and its goal is to placate the ghosts by satisfying that demand.

Dani Explanations for the Secular Phase   The Dani explain the secular phase of war as the result of many unresolved trouble cases between confederations. The secular phase does not actually resolve these cases, but it is a way of exacting revenge and it is such a bloody event that it overwhelms the minor grievances of the past.

Ethnographic Analysis of Factors Involved in the Ritual and Secular Phases

Topography   The flat valley floor allows dense populations and easy access of people to a battle.

Population Density   The high population density of the Grand Valley increases the potential for interpersonal conflict.

Size of Social Groups   The large sizes of confederations (about 1000) and alliances (about 5000) means that many people can be involved in wars.

Weapons Technology   Dani weapons are fairly ineffective, although they do kill people. Bows and arrows are inaccurate and have a short range. Jabbing spears and, more recently, steel bush knives have even shorter ranges.

Individualism and Informal Leadership   The high degree of individualism and the lack of powerful formal leaders limit the effectiveness of groups in combat. It means that even when hundreds of armed men are present at a battle, there are no really concerted maneuvers.

Aggressiveness   The low level of aggressiveness in most Dani does much to modify the effects of Dani warfare.

Emergence of Leaders   Warfare is an important arena for rising leaders to prove themselves.

Ceremonialism   An effect of warfare is to increase the number of ceremonies. In addition to the specific war ceremonies, there are the especially elaborate funerals for men killed in war. With increase in ceremonies comes increase in exchange and consumption of pigs and circulation of shelter valuables.

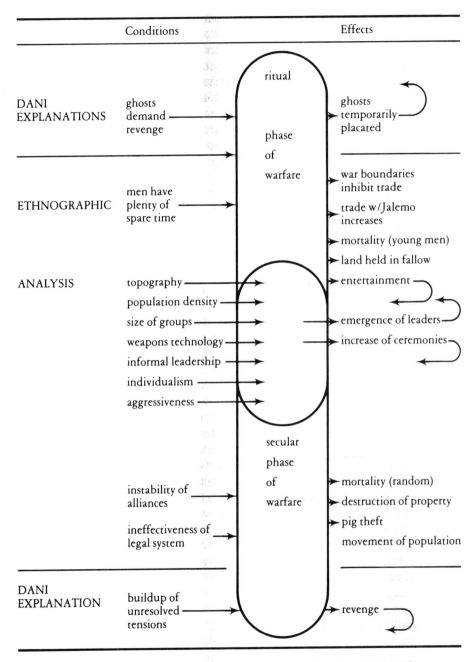

	Conditions	Effects

DANI
EXPLANATIONS   ghosts demand revenge → ritual ——— ghosts temporarily placated

ETHNOGRAPHIC   men have plenty of spare time →

phase of warfare

war boundaries inhibit trade
trade w/Jalemo increases
mortality (young men)
land held in fallow

ANALYSIS   topography →
population density →
size of groups →
weapons technology →
informal leadership →
individualism →
aggressiveness →

entertainment
emergence of leaders
increase of ceremonies

secular phase of warfare

instability of alliances →
ineffectiveness of legal system →

mortality (random)
destruction of property
pig theft
movement of population

DANI
EXPLANATION   buildup of unresolved tensions → revenge

Diagram 8.   Holistic summary of warfare. (Heider 1970:126)

Ethnographic Analysis of Factors Specific to the Ritual Phase

Spare Time   Battles and raids take time, and even more time is used up in guarding against enemy raids. However, for the men subsistence activities demand little time, so there is plenty of spare time for warfare.

Inhibition of Trade   Trade cannot take place across war boundaries; but war does not totally disrupt trade within the Grand Valley, for there are always ways to get around the battlelines. Since the most important source of salt in the Grand Valley is controlled by Gutelu, anyone at war with his alliance is at a disadvantage, but they can still get salt by trading with neutral middlemen.

Increased Trade with the Jalémo   The Jalémo, a lightly populated valley system to the northeast of the Grand Valley, is a source for many of the materials needed in war: fine straight wood for spears, as well as cockatoo and bird-of-paradise feathers and marsupial furs for ornaments. Thus, warfare in the Grand Valley stimulates trade with the Jalé.

Mortality   The deaths in the ritual phase of war occur almost exclusively among 15–25-year-old men.

Fallow Land   During wartime a 1- or 2-kilometer-wide strip of land between hostile alliances is left uninhabited, a dangerous no-man's-land which is the scene of battles and raids. Usually, some of this land is garden land, kept in enforced fallow until alliance boundaries shift.

Entertainment   Battles and raids do provide entertainment for the men.

Ethnographic Analysis of Factors Specific to the Secular Phase

Instability of Alliances   Because of the great individual strength of their member confederations, the alliances are inherently unstable groups.

Ineffectiveness of the Legal System   The inability of the legal system effectively to resolve conflicts between men of different confederations contributes to the buildup of tensions.

Mortality   The result of the secular phase of war in the 1966 instance (and probably in most) was a massive slaughter of men, women, and children concentrated in one small area.

Destruction and Looting   The secular phase is marked by considerable arson and looting.

Movement of Populations   After the secular phase of war, populations shift in order to open new protective no-man's-lands and to occupy old no-man's-lands.

Diagram 8 is a summary description of the place of war in Dani life. It is not a complete contextualization, of course, but it shows the more important strands which relate warfare to other aspects of life. It does not try to trace out all the effects—for example, the ritual phase kills off young men, which disturbs the balances of the marriage pools, thus allowing polygyny without bachelorhood (see p. 83). Nor does it try to weigh the different factors against one another—for example, having spare time to fight and sit in watchtowers contributes to the form of Dani warfare, but is not nearly as important as the Dani beliefs in ghosts, or the shortcomings of the Dani legal system.

Although it is analytically useful to distinguish between factors which the Dani themselves talk about and other factors which are only teased out of the data by ethnographic analysis, it should be noted that both sorts of factors have their own reality.

Finally, this diagram is like a piece snipped out of a very complex network. Many strands are left hanging when they should be doubled back to indicate the complex feedback nature of the system. Thus, an effect of war is that leaders emerge, but often those new leaders encourage war to validate their influence. Likewise, the massacre of 1966 resolved many old grievances for Mabel's men, but if left Um'ue's people with new grievances of their own against Mabel which will be worked out somehow. Such feedback loops are indicated in the diagram.

The advantage of the diagram and of the holistic analysis itself is obviously not that it gives an elegant description of cause and effect, but that it preserves some of the extremely complex cultural system in which Dani warfare is embedded.

Pacification

The Dutch government had been trying to end Dani fighting in the Grand Valley since 1958, and had achieved some success in the southern region around their main police post. In September 1961 they established peace between the Gutelu and the Widaia. The peace was broken by the massacre of 1966, but otherwise it held up well, supported of course by the force of armed police. In 1963 when the Indonesians took over from the Dutch, military units augmented the police.

There were sporadic outbursts of secular warfare from time to time despite the government, but the ritual phase of war did not resume. The continuation of the secular phase is understandable when one considers the main motivational factors for the Dani: The unresolved conflicts, which had been a causal precondition for the secular phase, continued to mount up. Neither Dutch nor Indonesians were able to institute a legal system which could deal with Dani trouble cases any more effectively than the old Dani system did. In a sense this inability is ironic, for both Dutch and Indonesians were familiar with effective higher-level legal systems, but both governments had focused on other aspects of Dani behavior and so neglected this one. In any case, they did not eliminate secular warfare; they only made it more costly for the Dani with armed punitive raids.

But the ritual phase of war—that long and impressive set of actions, sanctioned by the supernatural and thoroughly intermeshed with so much of Dani life—was stopped. I have already described my surprise that the Dani took pacification with such calm. I was surprised in part because I had equated violence (of which there was plenty in Dani warfare) with aggressiveness (which is rare for the Dani). If anything, fighting was anomalous, for it was inconsistent with the basic patterns of Dani life. It was not only not necessary to the Dani, but as it turned out, it was easy for the Dani to give up.

There was a second reason for my surprise at Dani reaction to pacification. Although Dani warfare was very widely interrelated with many other traits, when it was ended it seemed to make little immediate differences to their way of life. Men still spent their time sitting around talking, although no one had to sit alone atop the watchtowers. Frequent occasions were still found to eat pigs. One could use a physical metaphor and say that Dani warfare was widely based but shallowly rooted in their culture.

4 / Religion and Ritual

THE SUPERNATURAL

Mogat—*the Ghosts*

The Dani believe that when people die something called *mogat* leaves their bodies, but the *mogat* does not go far away. It tends to stay near the relatives of the deceased persons, in familiar territory. Human in form, a *mogat* can sometimes be seen and often is heard as it does humanlike things. In short, we have no trouble translating *mogat* as ghost.

Dani ghosts do both good and evil. They can help out in war by watching for enemy raids or by making an enemy man vulnerable to death in battle. But on the whole, ghosts are more malevolent than useful. When a person is sick or has had an accident, or even when a pig is sick, people blame the ghosts. If ordinary care does not bring about a cure, then people will perform a ceremony for the ghosts. When a person dies, much of the funeral has the explicit aim of placating the ghost. The activity, the feasting, and the gift exchange which are part of ceremonies are all done for the benefit of the ghosts, and the leaders of the ceremony frequently shout this news to the ghosts. A second goal of the funeral is to drive the ghost of the dead person away from where people live, to send it out into the forests. When a person has been killed in war, his ghost is particularly likely to cause misfortune, and must be placated not only by a large funeral but, later, by the death of an enemy.

Ghosts generally lurk around the compounds at night and make it dangerous for people to move about in the dark. However, ghosts are not believed to hurt children or pigs "because they feel sorry for them." Countless adults have told me about their narrow escapes from ghosts when they were foolish enough to go outside after dark—but these stories were usually told with a humorous twist and definitely not as tales of terror. Everyone agrees on how ghosts operate: They come up to a person from the front and throttle him with both hands. In fact, this throttling is used as a nonverbal gesture meaning "ghost." Often when I would ask something like why people did not go out at night, or what would happen if they did not obey the incest norm, my informant would answer simply by putting both hands to his throat, sticking out his tongue, and popping his eyes in a mood which was casually humorous, not terrified.

Ghosts eat food, and in most ceremonies food is set out for them, as the leader of the ceremony calls out in a very matter-of-fact, almost demanding voice, "You eat this!" Usually, if the food is pork, a person will eventually eat the ghosts' share. Sometimes people do the eating for ghosts during the ceremony. But for all that is done on behalf of the ghosts, little is ever actually sacrificed to them.

The Dani build various enclosures around the neighborhood to lure the ghosts and to keep them away from people. There are little houses along the war frontier and other sorts of enclosures in the forests; there is a "ghost house" in the compound behind every important men's house; and in the men's houses there are places for the ghosts to sit and even a false hearth for them to light their cigarettes.

I spent a lot of time trying to work out a systematic version of Dani ghosts, but it was a frustrating enterprise. All Dani know about ghosts and talk about them freely, but they do not worry about questions like how the same ghost can be on the frontier and in the compound and in the forests at the same time. The Dani really do not take their ghosts all that seriously. They are not pious believers. Certainly, everyone knows about ghosts, talks about them, and believes that they exist. And certainly, much is done in the name of the ghosts: Pigs are killed, ceremonies are held, wars are raged. Yet time and time again I saw evidence that the Dani were believers only as long as it was convenient.

When we first set up the expedition camp at Homuak, many of the young men would hang around to watch us, trying to talk with us; and in the evenings when dark fell, there would be little crises. The men would want to go home, but could not because of the ghosts—unless they could use our flashlights. For the first few nights we loaned our flashlights, but our battery supply soon threatened to give out. Finally, we declared that there would be no more flashlights. Some people left at dusk that day, but others stayed to test our resolution. It was sorely tried. There were some eloquent descriptions of what would happen to them without flashlights. Even with our one week of Dani we could understand what was being said. We held firm, and a few of the younger boys spent that first night in our tents. For a few days after that we had disgruntled neighbors, but soon Homuak was again a favorite evening meeting place. People came, stayed, walked home through the dark, and we heard no more of the necessity for flashlights.

One day after I had been there long enough to have worked out the sequence of funeral events, I was sitting with Um'ue and some other men in his men's house. It was raining. We were in the midst of a funeral, and I knew that this was the day when the men were supposed to comb the fields for rodents which were to be roasted in a special ceremony. But no one was moving. Finally, I asked Um'ue when things would begin. He looked once more out at the cold rain and said, "Never mind, it's too wet. We'll just cancel it this time."

A final example of their casual attitude toward ghosts: When war was going on in 1961, people said it was necessary because of the ghosts. But after the Dutch pacified the area, there was no more talk about the ghosts demanding war. The basic principle of Dani religion is: Ritual is undertaken to placate the ghosts. But there is an informal subclause to this principle: The threat of Dani ghosts adapts itself to the means available to placate that threat. Therefore, war was necessary until the Dutch guns made it inadvisable. On the whole, it is a very reasonable ghost system, adapting itself to the convenience of the people.

In addition to the ghosts, there are various spirits which inhabit certain hills, rocks, ponds, and whirlpools in streams. These are not the ghosts of dead people, and are not said to be anthropomorphic. Many informants told me of these spirits in some detail, with particular names, places of residence, habits (especially whether well- or ill-intentioned toward people), and often the name of a man who in some sense controlled that spirit. I was pleased with the first such list I got but dismayed when the second list (and subsequent ones) were just as detailed but differed in most of the details. This same gross disagreement had turned up in the realms of sweet potato names and stone adze words. Those items were nicely tangible, and I have already described the investigations which I pursued to try to clear up those problems (see p. 32). But I did not work on the spirit lists, and I can offer no good explanation for the disagreements.

The Edai-egen

A second concept basic to understanding Dani religion is *edai-egen.* Each person has an *edai-egen.* Although it is not itself supernatural, it is the target for ghostly attacks. The word *Edai* is used for the two-day dance which celebrates or announces the killing of an enemy; it also is the word for the songs sung during that ceremony. The word *Egen* is used in many contexts meaning "seed" or "essence." In his film *Dead Birds,* Robert Gardner translates *edai-egen* as "seeds of singing," which is what it is all about. I prefer "soul matter," for it indicates more literally what the Dani mean. They call the heart the *edai-egen* (a pig's heart is also called *edai-egen*), and it is the locus of human reasoning.

Children are born with *edai-egen.* As they slowly become independently human, and are able to walk and talk, their *edai-egen* grows and settles into its normal place in the chest just below the sternum. By the time a child is three or four, it has a fully adult *edai-egen.* Later in life, if a person has suffered any weakening through disease or wounds, people say that the *edai-egen* has gotten small and has moved to the backbone. This weakness is illustrated by a graphic nonverbal gesture: rotating the clenched fist just beneath the sternum. But this twisting of the *edai-egen* is done by the ghosts, so curing ceremonies are supposed to drive away the ghosts as well as restore and revive the *edai-egen.* Thus, the well-being of a person lies in the state of the *edai-egen,* and that can always be threatened by malevolent ghosts of old friends and relations who have been neglected. Most people wear some sort of charm to protect their *edai-egen* from ghosts.

Wusa—*Sacred Power*

Anything which has magical powers is *wusa.* One often hears the word in connection with ritual life. *Wusa* is power, and it can be dangerous to people if it is not handled with care. Corpses, for example, are *wusa,* as are war trophies and the sacred stones of a sib. When people have to handle such things, they usually cleanse themselves afterward by waving a feather over their hands to "cut the *wusa.*" Special places are *wusa,* and the knotted grass signs warning people away are *wusa.* Forbidden things are *wusa:* It is *wusa* to eat one's sib bird; it is *wusa* for a husband and wife to have sexual intercourse within five years after the birth of a child. In short, anything which has to do with ghosts involves this *wusa.* But as usual, generalizations about the Dani are tricky. For example, almost every time after a man has been working on a shell band for a funeral gift, he will find a feather to "cut the *wusa*" before he eats or smokes. But several times I have watched as a man who had no feather handy just skip that ritual and eat anyway.

People also casually extend the concept of *wusa* beyond the sacred: When someone wants to keep people from urinating near a compound or wants to mark a stack of lumber as his own, he will use the grass knots to keep people away. In such a case there is no claim that ghosts are involved, but *wusa* symbols are used anyway. Parents will even use the word to scold their children: When an infant has strayed too close to a fire or has made a complete mess of a woman's netting, she may gently move it aside saying, "Don't. That is *wusa.*"

The Sun and the Moon

The sun is a woman, usually called *mo,* but very occasionally when I was asking about it, someone would refer to it as *ninakoja,* "our mother." Some people say that she wears men's ornaments and carries a spear (as Dani women do in the *edai* dance). The sun spends the nights in a special house in the Pass Valley, a side valley entering the Grand Valley at the northeastern edge of the Gutelu Alliance. In the day the sun passes across the sky, and then at night retraces her steps to get back to her house. I tried to work out the mechanics of all this, but I could find no one who was concerned about details of how she would get home without being seen. Um'ue suggested that perhaps during her eastward trip she sat on a mat, thus blocking out her light, but this explanation may have been ad hoc ingenuity on his part rather than an authentic Dani conception of the sun.

The Pass Valley, where the sun spent the night, was always a mysterious-sounding place. An American army plane had crashed there on a sightseeing trip at the end of the Second World War, and there had been a dramatic rescue of the three survivors, duly reported in *Readers' Digest.* But the valley was isolated enough to discourage casual visitors. I eventually managed to have Gutelu escort me in to see the sun's house. It was a square structure of moderate size on stilts, with a bark roof, quite unlike anything else in the entire Grand Valley region, but similar to dwellings elsewhere in the New Guinea highlands. Gutelu did not allow me to look inside the house, but he said that it contained the skirts, ornaments, and weapons which the sun used.

The moon is a man, but beyond this no one agreed about its behavior, its relation (and possible kinship) to the sun, or even the names for the different phases. The moon is not important in Dani life or symbolism, although people do welcome the nights when the full moon makes it possible for them to move around freely.

Stars, also, are not important to the Dani. They do not even perceive them in groups or constellations. This casual attitude toward the heavens would be quite surprising in other areas, but the Dani in the Grand Valley need little information from the skies. Because there are no seasonal activities, there is no practical necessity to observe and anticipate solstices, equinoxes, or moments when the sun passes directly overhead. And since the Dani spend their lives within the familiar mountain-rimmed bowl of the Grand Valley, they do not need stars for navigation.

They do say that the brightest stars or planets are the heads of certain Big Men touching the sky, and people will point out one and name it after the Big Man in that direction. However, they do not observe closely enough to realize that stars and planets wander across the sky.

Myths

Myths are not important to the Dani; at least, myths are not widely known or told. It is always possible that there is a rich mythology which I never learned about, but I feel fairly safe in saying that this is most unlikely. The Dani have such a casual attitude toward all things sacred that it would be very surprising if myths were an exception. Myths are a sort of speculation, a way of organizing the unknown and filling in history, all of which the Dani are not particularly interested in. Finally, when I did get Um'ue to tell me about the mythology which he knew, it was almost by accident after I had stumbled across the key words.

As soon as we arrived in the Grand Valley, we heard from missionaries about Bird and Snake; and when I learned some Dani, I began asking people about it. There was a particular phrase basic to this myth: "My skin, your skin." But when I translated it into Dani I got no response. Even Um'ue denied knowing anything about it. I asked him several times, but with no luck. Then one day, many months later, someone brought in a dead snake. It was actually the only snake which I ever saw in the Grand Valley, and I took that opportunity to ask all manner of questions about it. Someone gave me in passing the word for skin, *abutal.* I was surprised. I knew that the word for skin was actually *oadlo.* I challenged my informant, but he held firm: "On people, and pigs, and sweet potatoes it is *oadlo,* but on snakes it is *abutal.*" That was one of those nice moments when insight flashed. I went looking for Um'ue, dragged him off, and said, "Tell me about *nabutal-habutal.*" "Oh," he said, "That!" And he proceeded to tell me.

Um'ue was, in that favorite ethnographic phrase, "my best informant." I think that he was extremely conscientious most of the time but as this incident suggests, he always made me work for my information. It was never possible to get him started on a story of this sort. I had to drag it out, detail by detail. So the following is not really a pure Dani text. (This also suggests that for all their verbal skill, Dani do not customarily tell this myth as public recital.)

The Myth of Bird and Snake

Snake and Bird had an argument about death. Snake held that people die, are cremated, and return to life (*nabutal-habutal*). Bird argued "No, that is not good. They should stay dead, and I'll smear mud on myself and mourn in sympathy." At this point Nakmatugi (the first man) settled the argument by saying, "I don't like snakes." And so men die, and birds mourn.

The phrase *nabutal-habutal,* "my (snake) skin—your (snake) skin," is important here for it links the idea of human immortality to the skin of the snake. Um'ue did not expand on the implications of this, and since snakes are so rare in the Grand Valley, it is not likely that other Dani could. But elsewhere in New Guinea and adjacent islands one finds similar mortality myths which explicitly state that the snake is immortal because it can shed its skin (see Heider 1970:144). This mysterious rejuvenation, so impossible to a human, is a widespread theme of myth.

Some Protestant missionaries in the Western Dani area used the phrase from the comparable Western Dani myth to translate the Christian concept of immortality in Jesus. (There is a constant problem in translating the Bible into a language like Dani: One needs to use concepts like "immortality," but is it better to take over the nearest Dani term or to invent a new word which has no pagan connotations?) In this case, pink-skinned North Americans told brown-skinned Dani that they would find *nabutal-habutal* in Jesus. Some Dani took the term in the literal sense and tried to achieve salvation by constantly washing and scraping themselves in rivers, hoping to change their skins (see O'Brien and Ploeg 1964). This all happened in the Western Dani region, but the myth is the same and the potential for confusion exists in the Grand Valley.

The Grand Valley Dani do not ponder much about their mortality or the immortality which they might have had, but another aspect of this myth does appear often in Dani life: the association of man with bird, which is expressed in the theme of Man-As-Bird. In Um'ue's version of the myth, men die (that is, the snake loses) because man dislikes snakes. In another

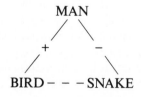

version, the bird wins because man is like birds, and birds die. The result is the same: In terms of death, man is like birds and both are different from snakes.

This triad, or parts of it, are found in mythology throughout the world. Most commonly man is associated with bird; where snakes appear in myth, they are almost always hostile to man; and sometimes the third leg, the conflict between bird and snake, is dramatized (as in the Aztec motif incorporated into the Mexican flag).

One does not have to be a believer in Jungian symbols to appreciate the power of the Dani myth. But except in the myth, snakes are rarely seen or thought about.

The bird is an important symbol to the Dani, however. We have seen how important the bird is in the mortality myth. There is another myth in which bird and man are associated:

The Separation of People from Animals

The people came out of the Huwainmo Cave, together with the *due* (birds, bats), *wato* (insects, reptiles, amphibians), and the *bpake* (forest mammals). The people and the birds were together, and the forest mammals were their pigs. Then they asked Nakmatugi who they were. He said, "You are people, you are birds, you are *bpake,* you are *wato.*"

Then the birds said, "We don't like the people, we'll go off and be birds." And the *wato* said the same, and the *bpake* said the same.

(from Heider 1970:141)

Although in the story birds are separated from man, the point of the myth is to establish a link between certain species of birds and certain human sibs. This is a classic totemistic relationship, and people are not allowed to eat the bird of their sib.

The theme of Man-As-Bird is obvious in ceremonies. The particular bird of the mortality myth is said to be the *ebe bulok,* "the little robin chat," which is black with white epaulets. People say that it was once completely black, but when it went into mourning for man's deaths, it smeared its shoulders with white clay. For battles, *edai* dances, and funeral ceremonies, both men and women smear light-colored clay on their shoulders in explicit imitation of the robin chat's markings. The feathered ornaments and the cassowary-feather dance whisks also recall the bird in the myth, as does the use of the bird call for battle. Sometimes at an *edai* dance, women or men dance in place, bending their knees and flapping their arms like wings, in explicit imitation of birds.

An even more obvious equating of man and birds is in the names for the war trophies, those weapons and ornaments taken from killed enemies and displayed at *edai* dances. In the Dugum Neighborhood they are usually called *ab watek,* "dead men," but in the southern Grand Valley they are *sue watek,* "dead birds." That is the title which Robert Gardner chose for his film on the Dani, of course, and he structured the film around the symbolic association of man and bird.

Witchcraft

While war deaths are attributed to collaborative efforts between the ghosts who prepare the way and the spears and arrows which finish the job, ordinary deaths are attributed to a combination of witchcraft and natural causes. That is, if I asked how someone died, the first answer would always be an obvious material/medical one: sickness, old age, or something like that. A frequent answer was *munu,* which refers specifically to head colds but seemed to be extended to nearly any bodily ailment. If I then pressed and asked how the person got *munu,* or whatever, people would eventually attribute it to the work of a witch.

The Dani of the Dugum say that they do not know how to perform witchcraft, but their neighbors do. The people to the south—the Widaia and beyond—kill by sprinkling a white powder in someone's sweet potatoes, and there are people to the north who kill by pointing a stick at their victims. Most of these witches are women. I was told that two women living in the Dugum Neighborhood who had come from the North were well-known as witches. As far as I could tell these women were quite ordinary, but after several deaths I began waiting for people to take some action against them, especially when I heard stories from Denise O'Brien about how the Western Dani hunted out and killed suspected witches there. The witchcraft patterns seemed almost identical in both areas with one great exception: The Grand Valley Dani did not seem to care. Belief in witchcraft was certainly general but there was no anxiety about it. I also have no idea whether anyone ever actually practiced witchcraft.

The habit of accusing people far away of being witches is familiar in the anthropological literature, and so the Dugum response was not surprising. But in 1968 when I went to live at Jibiga, in that northern region, I fully expected those people in turn to deny any practice of witchcraft and to blame the people of the Dugum. Instead, they proudly acknowledged that they were the experts and that the people in the Dugum did not know anything about the subject.

Ganekhe—*Sacred Objects*

Each man has some especially sacred objects called *ganekhe* which he keeps in a cabinet in the rear of a men's house. Most men deposit their *ganekhe* together with those of other men of their sib who live in the general area, but there is no specific rule that all sib members in a locality must keep their *ganekhe* together. (As I worked out the *ganekhe* groups, I sometimes thought that there was a sort of lineage grouping, where closely related men, with common descent, would keep their *ganekhe* together, but there always turned out to be too many exceptions for this to be true.) The men who have a set of *ganekhe* in one place sometimes join in a ceremony to renew the sacred power of the objects. Thus, they do constitute a group which can be called a local sib segment.

The *ganekhe* includes, first of all, small flat slate stones called *habo.* They are similar in form to the *je* (exchange stones), but unlike *je* they are very sacred and are never publicly displayed. At some ceremonies the *habo* are taken from the cabinet, unwrapped, and wiped with pig grease to renew them.

Other objects are stored in the cabinets and are considered part of the *ganekhe.* Among these are especially sacred bamboo knives which are brought out to carve pig skins at funerals. (Dani also frequently use smaller bamboo knives which are not at all sacred.) One man once showed me a collection of human mandibles which were in his *ganekhe,* but he either would not or could not tell me anything about them.

FUNERALS

The Dani have funerals to cremate a corpse and to placate the ghost and drive it away from the houses of the survivors. Funerals are a time for all those who were affected by the loss to come together to reaffirm their ties and begin the job of restoring the social network which has been torn by the death.

These are the usual functions of funerals, the sorts of tasks which every society must undertake when a person dies: disposal of the corpse and restoration of the supernatural as well as social worlds. What is unusual about the Dani funerals is their elaboration in time. Dani funerals are not particularly grand, but each funeral runs through a regular course lasting several years, from the time of death until the next Pig Feast.

The Cremation

When a person dies, the word is quietly sent out by messengers, and the next day the funeral begins in the dead person's compound. People come from all over a confederation and sometimes from the far reaches of an alliance and beyond. Before the cremation, however, a huge feast is cooked and eaten, and the funeral gifts are exchanged.

Throughout the morning people arrive singly or in small groups. With each arrival there is loud singing of a sort of dirge, the words drawn out in a mournful chant. The newcomers step inside the courtyard, and are recognized by the man running the ceremony, who stands at the men's house at the opposite end of the yard. The dirges are sung back and forth, and the men take a very stylized pose: standing with the weight on one leg, the other bent forward, one hand rubbing up and down the calf of the bent leg, the other wiping tears from the tightly shut eyes. For a few minutes the men sing, bend, and rub, and then suddenly it is over. The atmosphere of deep

Cowrie shell bands brought as funeral gifts must be redistributed, and the important men decide who is to get what.

mourning is broken, and everyone switches to matter-of-fact normal tones and postures. The two groups meet and embrace; the newcomers hand over their goods; and everyone continues his activities.

Some men and boys are out chopping wood for the cooking fires and the funeral pyre, and they appear every so often with logs. Other men scrape out the old steam pit and prepare the fire which will heat up the cooking rocks. Women have stopped off at their current sweet potato gardens and arrive with nets full of sweet potatoes. There is work to be done but many people share in it, and there is much visiting and cigarette smoking as the buildings and the courtyard itself slowly fill with people.

If the death was natural, then the corpse is kept inside the cook house or the men's house until the last moment. But if the person was killed in war, it is a "fresh-blood" funeral, and the corpse is set in a high sort of chair constructed in the middle of the courtyard for the purpose.

People bring shell bands, nets, pigs and sweet potatoes to the funeral. The shell bands and nets are draped over the corpse. Supposedly, men of the same moiety as the dead person's bring pigs, and people of the opposite moiety bring shell bands, but this principle is often violated. In a large fresh-blood funeral there can be more than 20 pigs and several dozen shell bands, in addition to miscellaneous gifts of feather ornaments, polished exchange stones, shell chest ornaments, and the like.

The pigs are assembled by late morning and the slaughter begins. Two men hold the pigs, one after the other, high in the air in front of the men's house. The leader of the funeral steps forward in an almost formal manner

At a funeral the Big Men discuss the redistribution of gifts.

and shoots a bamboo bladed arrow into the pig. No pig dies immediately. They run and stumble about, blood spurting from the wound. Sometimes they run through a group of seated visitors, and sometimes the men have to pursue a poorly shot pig and open up the wound with another arrow. The squealing is almost continuous until the last pig is killed and laid out in front of the men's house. Then the butchering can begin. Usually, several men and boys cluster around each pig, all working on it. The tails are saved to use as ornaments which protect against ghosts, and the rest of the pig is prepared for cooking.

Meanwhile rocks are being lifted onto a large fire. When the rocks are hot, everything is carefully packed together in the steam bundle. Women do most of Dani cooking, but at funerals and other important ceremonies the men step in and take over. It takes about an hour to build up the steam bundle. A round cone-shaped hole a meter and a half in diameter and about a meter deep is lined with grass. Then comes layer after layer of hot rocks, leaves and ferns, sweet potatoes, pork, whole pig skins, more rocks, and so forth, with water frequently poured on the rocks to make steam. The steam bundle starts in the pit, and is slowly built up until it is a stout column nearly head-high. It is finally wrapped in grass and leaves, tied by stout vines, and left to steam for another hour.

There is a lull in the pace of things while the steam bundle cooks. Then the men untie it and begin to pass out food—tubers, greens, and, more carefully, pork. Everyone gets some strips of pork. Each skin, heavy with its layer of fat, is held up and the leader of the funeral cuts it into strips with a broad bamboo knife. These strips are passed out to everyone, and they rub the fat over their bodies.

When people have eaten and the surplus food is packed away to be taken home, the shell bands are laid out on the ground. The most important men huddle around the display of bands, conferring about who is to get what. Some of the bands will be given to individuals, and some will be kept aside to form a memorial for the dead person. The leader of the funeral distributes the bands. He stands in the midst of the seated crowd, holding each band in turn above his head and shouting out the name of the recipient. The number of bands varies. At the funeral of an unimportant old man only four were distributed, but at the fresh-blood funeral of a young man there were nearly 40.

Funerals anywhere are a moment of reemphasizing the social ties, and they can be called rites of intensification. The Dani stress this aspect by passing the real objects, pigs and shell bands, along the links of their social network. At a funeral some people have brought pigs and all have shared in eating them; some have given shell bands, others have received them, and all have been witnesses.

The most important witnesses to the funeral, however, are the ghosts. In every way, explicit as well as implicit, the funeral acts shout out to the ghosts: "See this! See what we do for you!" And then, although this part is not so often said in words: "Now go away and leave us in peace!"

When the shell bands have been distributed, the central part of the courtyard is cleared. People crowd back against the houses. Some men lay a great square of logs to make the pyre. Others prepare the corpse. If it had been in a house, it is now brought out for the first time. If it had been in the courtyard on a chair, it is lifted off, the chair dismantled, and the planks added to the pyre.

The pyre is lighted, and as the fire begins to catch, the corpse is being greased for one last time. Then a few men pick it up, carry it the few paces to the pyre, lay it on top, and quickly build up the pyre with the last logs, hiding it from view. During this entire time everyone is dirging and perhaps a few of those closest to the dead person are shaking in deep and genuine grief. Once, a man who had lost his young wife in an epidemic went out of control and tried to follow her body into the flames; he had to be held back by his friends.

At the moment that the corpse is put on the pyre, two men start the process of sending the ghost away. One holds a bundle of grass high over the corpse. The other man strikes it and shouts to the ghost to come along, as he grabs the bundle and runs down the courtyard toward the entrance. If it was a war death, or an important man, he shoots an arrow into the bundle; otherwise he hits or stabs it with a club or spear. (Once in the evening after the funeral of a boy who had been killed in an enemy raid, they took this a step further. A man organized a dozen boys, who armed themselves with rocks. Then starting at the back end of the compound, they raced through it, shouting, and pelting houses and fences with the rocks, trying to drive the ghost away.)

By evening most of the visitors have left; the pyre has burned down to coals. The closest friends and relatives remain, and they stay up all night talking, joking, smoking, eating. Early in the morning before dawn, some of the young men go out to a hilltop and there, looking out toward the enemy, they wait for dawn and listen for sounds of the enemy.

Finger Mutilation

On the second day the remains of the bones are picked out of the ashes, wrapped in a banana leaf bundle, and hung on the cook house wall. Nets are distributed to the women in a way very similar to the handing out of the shell bands to the men the day before. Some people come, but not nearly as large a crowd as the day before, and another meal is prepared in a steam bundle.

But near dawn on this day, if it has been a fresh-blood funeral, an extraordinary step is taken to placate the ghosts: some young girls who were particularly close to the killed person have their fingers chopped off.

This is a normal Dani practice. Out of all the Dani women whom I saw, only two had not lost any fingers. One of these was deaf, and people said that because they had felt sorry for her when she was a girl, they did not chop off any of her fingers. The other I cannot explain at all. She was a girl in her early teens, whose father was not particularly important. People said merely that she had objected, and so they had not chopped off her fingers. No woman has lost all her fingers—all have at least their thumbs and the first two fingers on one hand, but many have no more than that.

Although I never actually saw the operation, many people described it vividly. Several girls are brought to the funeral compound early on the second day. One man, the specialist in this practice, is waiting for them. First he ties off a girl's arm with a tight string above the elbow. Then he smashes her elbow down on a rock or board, hitting the olecranon process, the "funny bone," in order to numb the nerves in the fingers. Someone holds the girl's hand on a board, and the man takes a stone adze and with one blow he cuts off one or two fingers at the first joint.

The wound is bandaged with leaves, and through the rest of the day the girl sits in a prominent place, quiet, probably in a state of shock, holding her wounded hand upright to begin its healing. Infections from this operation seem to be rare. Certainly, I never saw any develop.

As many as three girls between about three and six years old lose one or two fingers in a fresh-blood funeral, but a girl may participate several times.

The Dani say that this mutilation is necessary to placate the ghosts, and they compare it with the other funeral goods. This practice is the only real sacrifice connected with Dani ritual. Even the pigs which are killed are then distributed as food to the people at the funeral, and nothing is really destroyed on behalf of the ghosts. The severed fingers are put aside, and as far as I could tell, they have no particular power or value. So, in one sense, they are like shell bands and pigs which are supposed to communicate to the ghosts the concern of the living. But quite unlike pigs and bands, they are not part of the circulating wealth which emphasizes the social ties at a funeral.

One result of this girlhood sacrifice is that Dani women go through life with severely mutilated hands. It is worth noting, however, how skillful the women are despite this. They do many sorts of tasks, and they even use tools effectively. They knit the carrying nets, which is a fairly fine handicraft. I cannot think of any activities which in other cultures women normally do, but which Dani women cannot perform because of their mutilations. Only once did a woman mention such a thing: Um'ue's old mother once joked that she could not use the heavy man's digging stick because she had no fingers.

Of all things which the Dani do, chopping fingers off little girls is the hardest to come to terms with. In Robert Gardner's film *Dead Birds* there is a scene of girls who have just lost their fingers. They are sitting, staring, at a funeral. This scene has more impact on American audiences than any other. Whenever I show the film one of the first questions is usually about finger mutilation. Warfare is easy to understand. Even the secular phase, with its treacherous massacres of women and children, is familiar to Americans. But the deliberate mutilation of helpless and probably unwilling girls is another matter. It strains the anthropological principle of cultural relativity, but it also raises a more theoretical problem. This finger mutilation seems to be out of keeping with the rest of Dani culture. It is a painful and extreme thing done to little children because of the ghosts. Yet, in everything else, the Dani do not go to extremes for their ghosts, and they rarely cause great pain to anyone, especially to children.

The holistic approach, which is used here, describes various aspects of Dani life as parts of an interrelated context. Even in tracing out the interconnections, however, one must be careful not to fall into the trap of suggesting that everything is part of a beautiful organically functioning whole. Here I take a position of cautious holism. But then, is it possible to move from this position to say that a trait in a culture is incongruous with that culture? And how would one demonstrate the truth of such a claim?

There is now one important fact to be added to this account: In the mid-1960s the Dani of the Gutelu region gave up finger mutilation. There is an obvious explanation for this. Because after 1961 there was no more ritual phase of war, no more funerals focused on ghosts, and so the explicit Dani reason for mutilation was gone. I do not know how keenly the Dani worried about ghosts during the 1966 massacre and its aftermath, but apparently no fingers were chopped off then.

I would suggest, however, that we cannot satisfactorily account for finger mutilation by putting it into the context of current Dani culture. Rather, it seems to have long-forgotten roots and has somehow survived, perhaps changing, perhaps growing, with its own momentum, as a trait unquestioned by the Dani and quite discordant with the general pattern of their culture.

Another trait disappeared under what may have been similar circumstances. All the while I was doing fieldwork in the Grand Valley, I made it a practice to go off wandering by myself exploring the countryside—partly to make up for the Dani interest in telling me things out of the blue. I often discovered things which I could later ask about and fill in important gaps in my knowledge. Among the curious findings from these explorations was the fact that there were human bones scattered in nearly half a dozen places over the Gutelu Alliance, in hollow trees, in rock ledges, and in caves. This was especially curious, since now the Dani cremate their own dead and return corpses of enemies to their own people (thoroughly booby-trapped with magical devices, of course). People always said that these stray bones were just the remains of unfortunate travelers who had died or been killed deep in the territory and had been left to rot. But one day I found a collection of human long bones with what seemed to be regular adze marks on them. These cuts looked very much like butchering marks left on animal bones. I brought the matter up with Um'ue who said yes, they did eat human flesh, but they then gave it up when his father was young (I estimated in the mid-1930s). Um'ue could give me no reason for ending it. It would have been either before European contact or around the time of the brief visit in 1938 by the American Museum of Natural History Expedition which camped at the other end of the Valley and could hardly have had any influence here. But Um'ue's story seems plausible, and the bones corroborated it. There are references to cannibalism in the origin myth; missionaries may have witnessed it in the southern Grand Valley in the 1950s (see Hitt 1962:126); and Koch has reported cannibalism with certainty from the Jalé, or eastern Dani, in the 1960s (Koch 1970).

At any rate, finger mutilation, like cannibalism, has disappeared from Grand Valley Dani culture.

The Next Days

For the next three days the funeral continues. Each day another steam bundle is made, but now there are only a few guests from the immediate vicinity. The ashes of the dead person are dumped into a small enclosure behind the men's house. A new carrying net is prepared and decorated with all the pigs' tails which had been removed during the first day of the funeral. This net symbolizes the dead person, and will figure in later stages of the funeral.

The End of the Mourning

Some weeks after the cremation the second stage of the funeral takes place in the same compound as the first. It is as big an event as the first part, and sometimes even more pigs are brought to be slaughtered. For three days steam bundles are made, and people gather and feast. All this is supposed to placate ghosts, but even more importantly, it is held for the benefit of the closest survivors. People said that the various events were to revive the *edai-egen,* the "soul matter," of those who had been grieving for the dead person. Boys put on new penis gourds; women who have been wearing plain skirts since the cremation replace them with their own decorated marriage skirts; and men, for the first time since cremation, now pluck off their moustaches.

The main ceremony takes place on the second day around an arch of sugar cane. A man reaches his hands through the arch holding roasted pork, steamed sweet potato, and a length of sugar cane. The mourners each come forward, take a bite of the three foods, chew for a while, and then spit it out, as a Big Man shouts the name of the dead person, calling to the ghost, saying, "You eat!" Blood from the pigs is smeared on the palms, elbows, knees, and head of each person to further restore them.

Carrying the Je Stones

The first two parts of the funerals were done for each individual death, and I saw them many times. But they are not the end of ritual concern with a death. There are two subsequent ceremonies which bring together all the funerals and in which larger groups are involved. In the first two parts people attended and participated because of their relationship to that particular dead person. The last two parts are held by the entire society, and deal with all the deaths which have occurred within the past few years. I observed the first two parts enough times to be able to make a generalized description of the behavior. But these last two parts I saw only once, and although I can describe each event, I cannot vouch for the general validity of the description of these parts. I cannot separate out the unique accidental from the normative.

In October 1961 the Wilihiman-Walalua, together with two other closely associated confederations of the Gutelu Alliance, held a ceremony called "carrying the *je* stones," in memory of the recent deaths in these confederations.

During the two days there was great activity throughout the area. People were assembling cowrie shell bands, women's carrying nets, and the large exchange stones called *je*. The *je* are flat slate stones ranging in length from 20 to 70 centimeters. They are often decorated with lengths of woman's skirt material, fur tufts, parrot feathers, and sometimes red ochre lines painted against the dark stone. The *je* are valuable but they are not *wusa,* or sacred, and during this part of the funeral they are constantly displayed, even while they are being carried from one compound to another.

Probably even more goods are involved in this exchange than were brought to the individual cremations held during the past years. At each compound where a cremation had been held months or years before, the leader of that funeral accumulates the gifts. The ideal pattern is that the *ami,* the men of the dead person's mother's sib and moiety, are responsible for contributing these goods. But in fact, I saw goods being brought also by men of the same moiety as the dead person; however, even in these instances the leaders of the funeral greeted and thanked them with the term "*ami.*" It was quite inappropriate as a kinship term, but it did signify that they, like *ami,* were bringing shells and stones.

For each dead person there was a bundle of nets, some shell bands, and some *je* stones. By the end of the second day and in the morning of the third day, one could hear shouting everywhere as small parties set out for the compound where the mass ceremony would be held. Each group was made up of men, women, and children moving slowly along the paths, taking time to dance and sing. It was like a moving *edai* dance, coming together from all points to the one large focal compound.

The compound belonged to Sula, an old man of great importance who might once have rivaled Gutelu for influence within the Alliance. Even in this ceremony there were overtones of the political rivalry, for Gutelu and his closest associates were pointedly absent.

When everyone had arrived, the memorial bundles were carefully laid out in two long lines stretching down the length of Sula's compound. The compound itself was of extraordinary length, built to accommodate this ceremony. Each bundle was unpacked, the nets folded carefully and laid out in a long high pile. The *je* stones were laid across the nets, and then the cowrie shell bands were stretched along the lines of nets. I counted a total of 37 piles of nets and 167 exchange stones in all.

As soon as the goods were laid out, the buzz of noise from the hundreds of people suddenly quieted down. It was almost the only time in any Dani ritual where there was a central focus of attention. Even the most significant moments in other ceremonies had to be carried on over the conversation of an inattentive congregation. But now there was near silence. Old Sula came out of his men's house and looked down the lines of goods. Then slowly, he walked down the courtyard, stopping at each bundle. He touched it, shouted out the name of the dead person it symbolized, calling once again for the ghosts to recognize the concern of the living, to be satisfied, and to go away. As soon as Sula finished, the spell of sacredness broke abruptly. Everyone who had carefully laid out a bundle now quickly packed it up and left for home.

The next day, crowds gathered at compounds all over the three confederations. The bundles were again laid out and again important men shouted the names over them. Vegetables (but not pork this time) were steamed and everyone ate. The bundles were then hidden away in the rear of houses to wait for the next step of funerals, the great Pig Feast.

THE PIG FEAST

The Grand Valley Dani Pig Feast may well be the most important ceremony, relative to its culture, in the world. It is celebrated by an entire alliance once every five years or so. Then, and only then, into the space of two and a half weeks are packed all manner of important rituals: weddings, initiations, the final part of funerals, and ceremonies which have to do with affirmation of leadership and with warfare. It is hard to imagine that a society could load more ceremonial weight into one brief period of time.

From the moment that we arrived in 1961, we asked about the next Pig Feast, and were always told that it would begin soon. But we were to be disappointed. By the time that the other members of the Expedition had left, in August 1961, the Pig Feast seemed no closer. In October 1962 when I left for a six-month break, I was apprehensive that they might hold it while I was away. But when I returned in March 1963, only the first step had been taken. Two or three months earlier Gutelu, as the leader of the Alliance and therefore also of the Pig Feast, had put a ritual prohibition on the killing of any pigs in order to allow the herds to build up for the great slaughter which would take place at the Pig Feast.

As it happened, during the next months the prohibition was not even lifted for funerals. I saw only three funerals, one of an unimportant old woman and two of infants, and at none of them were pigs killed. I wondered what would have happened if an important person had been killed, but got no answer to this. People still ate pork whenever a pig happened to die, and I had a feeling that some of the pigs which were eaten then had died under suspicious circumstances. One pig had obviously been killed by a spear, but everyone explained that it had been done by ghosts and therefore was certainly no violation of Gutelu's prohibition.

In June 1963 the next step was taken to build up the pig herds. At one ceremony I watched as 67 male piglets were castrated and sprinkled with special water. Both acts were believed by the Dani to make the pigs grow larger for the Pig Feast.

In November 1963, on Thanksgiving Day, the dissident Wilihiman-Walalua and their friends tried to force Gutelu's hand with a ceremony announcing the imminent beginning of the Pig Feast. They all gathered once again at old Sula's compound and feasted. Then the Big Men dramatically carved up pig skins and sent runners carrying strips of skin and fat to all the alliances in the Grand Valley, saying that the Pig Feast was under way. Gutelu did not rise to the bait, and the Pig Feast did not begin. I finally had to leave the Grand Valley: I had extended my stay long enough, I was committed to be back at Harvard for the spring semester, and I had little faith in Pig Feasts anymore. However, in February 1964, two months after I had left, Gutelu did begin the Pig Feast. I read about it in the dissertation of Herman Peters, OFM, a Dutch missionary anthropologist.

But six years later, in February 1970, when I arrived back in the Grand Valley for my fourth visit, there was no question that the next Pig Feast was soon to begin.

The old Gutelu Alliance had been split by the 1966 massacre, of course. Um'ue and Obagatok, leaders of the new alliance to the south, had already held their Pig Feast. But in 1970 I was staying at Jibiga where Gutelu lived in the center of the old alliance area. By 1970 Mabel seemed to have taken over the leadership of the Alliance, but Gutelu was still a very dynamic charismatic figure. And Jibiga was still the center of activity and the focus of outside power: Within a kilometer of Gutelu's compounds were the Dutch Franciscan mission station, its school and airstrip, as well as an Indonesian police post on one side and an army camp on the other.

So finally, more than nine years after first coming to the Grand Valley, I was to see a Pig Feast (for a full description, see Heider 1972b). Around Jibiga preparations had been under way for months. A taboo had been placed on killing pigs, and all outstanding debts were being called in by notifying Dani in other parts of the Grand Valley and beyond that the Pig Feast was approaching. These preliminary steps were necessary to ensure that when the Pig Feast began there would be enough pigs.

Now it became clear who the leader of the Alliance was. The taboo was placed, and the notifications were sent out by Mabel, the brilliant young organizer of the 1966 attack. Gutelu, an old but still active man, was very much present. He supervised some events, but there was no doubt that the main leadership had passed to the younger man.

Through March and April the Dani prepared for the Pig Feast. Great quantities of firewood were cut in the high forests and brought to the compounds. Every day the mountain slopes behind my house thundered as young men tumbled logs downhill to the valley floor. Nearly every house was given a new thatched roof, and many were rebuilt. Men braided skirt material for their daughters' weddings, or prepared costumes for their sons' initiations. Marriages were arranged, and the incredibly intricate series of gift exchanges for marriages, initiations, and funerals were mapped out.

The Indonesian government and the Franciscan priest at Jibiga also took an interest in the arrangements. Some attempts were made to regulate or at least to pass on the marriages, but much was said and little understood by the Dani. The Dani practice polygyny, which was a problem for the Christians, but practically no Dani had been baptized. There was a feeling among the officials that girls should not marry at too young an age. But the Dani do not keep track of age, and girls marry at the first Pig Feast after puberty. There were some girls just on the line who would obviously be well past marriage age by the time of the next Pig Feast five or six years hence. The Dani thought that they should be allowed to marry, but the officials felt otherwise.

There were two relatively clear rulings: One, that no girl should be forced to marry against her will; and two, that any boy who married would have to leave school. Even the first rule was a bit ambiguous—it would be very difficult for a girl to ask support from the police or army against the wishes of her family. For the schoolboys the second rule posed a real problem. There were a dozen boys in the fifth grade, many of them in their late teens, just barely within the normal range for marrying. They were well on their way toward fluency in Indonesian. They were almost ready to move definitively out of Dani culture and take up positions in the pan-Indonesian society. If they married, they would relinquish all that and be totally committed to Dani life. They had been exposed to outsiders, especially the priests and schoolteachers, but I doubt that any of them had a clear idea of where that path led. They had seen one or two Dani police recruits and a Dani catechist, but they had never seen a Dani schoolteacher, priest, carpenter, government official, or police or army officer. On the other hand, even those who were houseboys for the mission had families nearby, and were still strongly embedded in daily Dani life. In the end, most of the older boys dropped out to get married, and the younger boys, who could not have married anyway, stayed on.

The Pig Feast began in earnest on May 1, 1970. For 17 days the entire Alliance was involved in ceremonies. Some 5000 people in dozens of compounds scattered over dozens of square kilometers of valley and mountain were celebrating weddings, initiations, and funerals. Hundreds, perhaps thousands, of pigs were killed and eaten by the people of the Alliance and their guests. Vast quantities of pigs and pork, of nets and cowrie shell ornaments changed hands, paying off debts incurred a generation before and setting up obligations which would take another generation to fulfill.

During those days I abandoned all my other research and followed the Pig Feast—or tried to follow it. So much was happening at the same time at different places that it would have taken a team of investigators to observe it all. Often the different strands merged into one: since each Dani is related to others in many different ways, parts of the same pig might be at once an

The leaders of a ceremony carve the steamed pig skin into pieces which will be handed out to the people present.

uncle's contribution to his sister's son's initiation, a father's contribution to his son's wedding, and a son's contribution to his father's funeral. In the great net of Dani society, each strand was being renewed with the fat of the Pig Feast, and old strands which had been removed by death were replaced by new ones woven that May.

But for all that, the Pig Feast was rarely dramatic. Many of the most significant moments were performed almost offhandedly, and were easily missed by the casual observer.

The best way to describe the Pig Feast is to disentangle the three major sets of ceremonies and treat each one in turn: wedding, initiation, and funeral.

Weddings

On May 5 the weddings began. These were the first weddings held in the entire Alliance since the last Pig Feast six years earlier. Each wedding establishes a new social bond between two kin groups. This social bond is marked by the giving of pigs which will continue for an entire generation. Most of the pigs are given by the groom's family to the bride's family: at the wedding, at a ceremony a couple of years later, when children are born, and when daughters are married. Thus, at any one wedding the groom's family gives pigs to the bride's father and brothers, and some of these pigs are passed on to the bride's mother's male relatives as part of a long-past wedding payment.

The wedding begins at the home of the bride as she is vested with the signs of womanhood: new carrying nets, a new digging stick, and most important, a woman's skirt. As a girl she wore the loose-hanging grass skirt. But now she stands in the cook house as her mother and the other women wind her woman's skirt around her waist. The skirt is made of some 30 yards of braided plant fiber, decorated with red and yellow orchid fiber. Winding the skirt is an art, for it must be held in place by pressure, not gravity. It does not ride easily above the hips, as a Western skirt does. One of the first questions of visitors to the Grand Valley is: "How do they keep their skirts on?" The answer seems to be: by careful winding and cautious movements. As each loop is made and adjusted, a tight band is built up at the top, and then the later loops are draped down in front and behind to cover the vital parts. This is the true wedding band, which a woman wears for life. Only sometimes will she take it off, or replace it with a cruder version when working in the gardens.

As the ceremony got under way the brides were just giggling girls, somewhat embarrassed at being the center of attraction, but they changed almost within minutes as the import of the day sank in. By late afternoon they were exhausted. Weighed down by their new nets, hobbled by their new skirts, stuffed with pork and glistening with grease, they sat against the wall of the cook house, quiet and perhaps still tearful. In some compounds several girls went through the day together, but in others each girl was alone.

Three brides, still wearing their girl's skirts, are draped with their wedding nets as their kinswomen mourn for them.

For the next days, as the Pig Feast continued around them, the new women slowly recovered. They had to learn to walk again. One would see them waddling around the courtyard, using their digging sticks as canes, learning to manage the strange new skirts.

Four days after the skirt windings, the brides were delivered to their husband's compounds. Each bride was escorted by a dozen or more women and girls who danced and sang around her as she made her slow way across sweet potato gardens to her new home. Once there, she was handed over to the women of her husband's household, and the others left quietly.

Dani weddings are clearly social relationships between two groups. Unlike weddings which emphasize the union of two individuals, the Dani emphasize the fact that a young woman has moved from one household to another. At this point she is a socioeconomic object, as the pigs which move in the opposite direction are economic objects. The groom plays no public part at all, and indeed it is not for a year or two that man and wife will have their own household and begin having sexual intercourse.

The transactions begun at a wedding are summarized in Diagram 9.

1. At the wedding during the Pig Feast, the groom's family sends pigs to the bride's family and receives the bride and her belongings.

2. Two years later, at another ceremony, the groom's family gives valuable objects to the bride's family, and they all feast on pigs which are furnished by the bride's family. This event also marks the time when the young couple can begin to have sexual intercourse with each other. In a technical sense, we can say that the economic and social services of the bride have been transferred earlier; now her sexual services are available to the groom. This two-year delay between the beginning of the wedding and its consummation is not surprising when one considers that the same people will enter a five-year postpartum sexual abstinence at the birth of each of their children (see p. 84).

3. When children are born, the mother's *ami* (often her actual mother's brother) gives shell goods and gets a pig.

4. and 5. This pattern is repeated when the child is initiated (if a boy), is married (if a girl), or dies.

Thus, at a wedding ceremony the idea pattern has a young man, the groom, giving pigs to his new father-in-law who in turn passes some of them on to *his* father-in-law as part of the wedding exchanges begun a generation earlier. There is also a further complication: The young groom is of the same moiety as the man who eventually winds up with his pigs, namely his wife's mother's father (or brother). Those two men, who stand at opposite ends of the pig transactions, are actually likely to be of the same sib, and even of the same neighborhood or compound. The economic value of a pig, or its potential as a meal, is quite overshadowed by its importance as a piece in this incredibly complex set of transactions which takes place during a Pig Feast. When one considers that during the 17 days of the Pig Feast many hundreds, perhaps thousands, of pigs are on the move throughout the Alliance, one has some slight glimpse of what the Pig Feast means to Dani Society.

The Initiation

I hesitate to call what the Dani do an "initiation." It is not a ritual which all boys go through to "become men." Instead, it reflects the moiety system, for only half the boys go through it to "become Waija." As described above

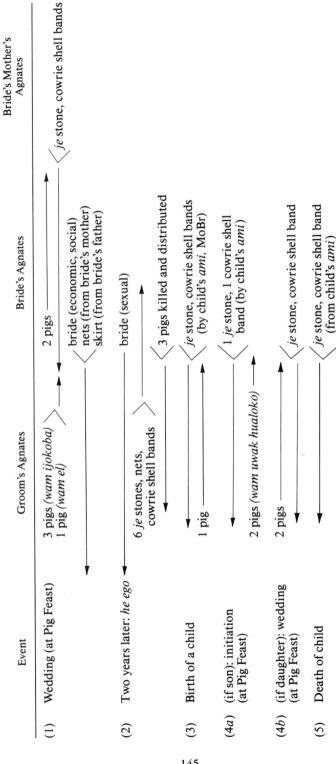

Diagram 9. Marriage-related exchanges.

(from Heider 1972b)

(see p. 69), every Dani is either of the Wida moiety or the Waija moiety, and can only marry a person of the opposite moiety. One gets one's membership from one's father, and so these are exogamous patrimoieties. Moiety systems are known from elsewhere in the world, but the Grand Valley Dani moieties have a unique aspect: All children are born Wida, whatever their father's moiety. Then at the first appropriate Pig Feast, those boys whose fathers are Waija all go through a ritual process which the Dani call *Waija hakasin* "to make them Waija." Their sisters just become Waija without ceremony. The Wida boys, of Wida fathers, have no comparable ceremony. The usual explanations of initiation focus on its social or psychological function of moving the boys dramatically from one status to another, or separating them from the woman's world and incorporating them into the men's world. But in the Dani case, the Wida men who have not participated in the initiation are no less men, or warriors, or Dani. So perhaps it is best to see the Dani initiation not in terms of its effect on the individual boys, but as a great social ceremony which underlines and reaffirms the basic moiety division of the society.

The initiation began on the first day of the Pig Feast. About 175 boys, ranging in age from 3 to nearly 20, took part. The age spread surprised me, but it was consistent with the general casualness of all Dani ceremonies. People explained that at the 1964 Pig Feast they used all the pigs for marriages, and there were not enough left for the initiation—so it had been 10 or 11 years since the last initiation. For those boys who had then been in the 3- to 8-year-old range, participation had been optional, and many had skipped it. But now they were all participating. The youngest of this year's initiates were led through the ceremonies by their fathers or older brothers, who often had to carry them or calm their crying. There was little in the way of hazing or physical abuse, but for the little boys only a year or two past the toddler stage, it was all a bit frightening.

The first step was to purify the boys, to remove the effects of all the taboo foods which they had eaten. They stood in a double line as a group of men went to each in turn, giving him a bit of pork to nibble and then to spit out. Four times the men made the round, and four times the boys nibbled and spit. The boys were made to stand straight so that the impurities could more easily flow out of their bodies.

The boys' part in the initiation was now suspended for 10 days, but the very next day some 50 men gathered in a fallow garden to build a compound which they called *Wusa-ma,* the "Sacred Place." Later the boys would be secluded here. The compound, with six houses, was built in hours. It was not as well constructed as usual, for the houses would be used only for four days and then abandoned.

On the tenth day, early in the morning, the boys were brought to the Sacred Place. Each boy wore an orchid fiber belt and a small red net, and carried weapons—bows decorated with yellow cockatoo feathers and arrows daubed with white lime. From each village cluster in the Alliance the

Gutelu, the old leader, with boys about to begin their initiation. (The man in the background is helping to run the initiation.)

boys approached, converging into larger and larger groups. Each group was escorted by men, singing, dancing, and carrying spears.

As they neared the Sacred Place other men ran ahead to hide in ditches; when the boys approached, they charged forward in noisy ambush. Each time the boys drew back, and their guardians faced the ambushers. After a short mock skirmish the ambushers disengaged and moved forward again to set up another ambush.

At the entrance to the Sacred Place a split sugar cane formed an arch, and two men clasped hands to form a second arch through which the boys passed to enter the compound. For the next four days the boys lived and slept in the Sacred Place. They were secluded, but hardly hidden, for the houses were in familiar territory, within sight of many of their own compounds and the mission post. Each morning they were taken outside to a grassy meadow where they rolled in the chilly dew, to cleanse themselves and "make them cold." They were fed only pig fat and taro, not the usual sweet potato, and all their food was cold.

On the second day of their seclusion there was a huge mock battle. The boys were led out to a field near the Sacred Place, and as they watched from a low hillock, their fathers and brothers—the Waija men—were attacked by an army of Wida men. This was the only time when Wida men participated in the initiation. I can only speculate what this battle signified: perhaps some long-forgotten historical event when Wida and Waija were separate tribes?

The mock battle was like the real battles which I had seen in 1961. The Indonesian government officials had agreed that it could be held if no real weapons were used. So the Dani shot untipped reeds and arrows, and used lengths of cane as spears. But very quickly they were carried away by their enthusiasm. Reeds and canes were joined by flying sticks and stones. Men began to limp back, bloodied, and a few minutes after it had begun, the Indonesians called a halt, firing their guns into the air.

On May 14, the final day of seclusion in the Sacred Place, the symbolism came thick and fast. The boys were led out to the meadow where they stacked their bows and arrows, danced, and waited. Then when all was ready, they were led single file to a hidden place in a stream bed where a long fire, covered with leaves, smoked away. The smallest boys arrived first, carried by their guardians. As each boy arrived he was thrown or pushed onto the fire. The screams were horrendous, but they were screams of surprise, not pain. The leaves dampened the flames, and the boys were well smoked but not burned. As the older boys arrived they threw themselves on the fire, shouting and rolling on it. Soon everyone, even the men, took his turn.

Then quickly the boys were led to a tall tree. Each was given a 4-foot-long reed spear with the tip bent back to make a hook. Each boy threw his spear into the tree. If it lodged in the branches, he would have many wives; but if it fell out, he would grow up to be a worthless, wifeless *gepu.* There was great laughing and jeering as one or another spear stayed or fell. But everyone had many tries, and eventually all the spears stayed.

Initiates are thrown on a fire to ritually restore their warmth at the end of the initiation ceremony.

Most Dani symbolism is quite implicit. The Dani themselves cannot—or will not—explain it, and I can only make my own guesses. But as I was watching the tree of spears and making the fairly obvious connection, Mabel came up behind me, jabbed my arm and pointed to the tree. "Do you know what that is?" he asked. I looked blank. No Dani ever volunteers this sort of information. "Women!" he laughed, making the nonverbal gesture of sexual intercourse with his fingers.

The boys moved on to the next event, the bamboo tubes. When I first came to the Grand Valley, missionaries had spoken of Gutelu's "book." It was most secret and sacred. Gutelu had bragged about it to them, but no one had seen it. Could it be some souvenir from the Archbold Expedition of 1938, or from the U.S. Army airplane crash of 1945? There was no native writing system in New Guinea, but bronze tools had been found on the coast, tying New Guinea in somehow to the Southeast Asian Bronze Age. After much pleading and some impressive gifts on my part, Gutelu agreed to show me his "book." We walked for many hours over the mountains, into a side valley, to the house where the sun spends the night—the most sacred place of all for the Grand Valley Dani. Here Gutelu brought out a small bundle, unwrapped it, and showed me his "book"—a 10-inch bamboo tube decorated with incised lines. I was intensely disappointed, but it was what I had bargained with to see: *holal Gutelu-mege, Gutelu's holal.* The word *holal* means the lines graved into the shaft of an arrow or onto a bamboo tube, and is now used to refer to our writing. So here was Gutelu's "book."

Now, eight years later, I saw many "books." The boys were lined up again, and in great secrecy the men unwrapped large bundles which contained dozens of the decorated bamboo tubes. Each boy was given one to hold in front of him, and in the open mouth of each tube was put a strip of white pig fat. Then using red ochre, the men made a red line down the forehead and nose of each boy. I had been waiting for this moment for years. Whenever I had asked about the initiation, all that people could or would tell me was about the red line on the boys' faces. I had speculated that this marking was somewhat analogous to the blood-drawing circumcision or other mutilations of initiations in other cultures. I had hoped that by seeing the red line in context and by being able to talk with people immediately afterward, I could learn more about the Dani views. But I had no such luck. The Dani were never eager to explain such things. Now with government officials, missionaries, anthropologists, and a Japanese-Indonesian television crew all watching and often intruding, they felt spiritually beleaguered. I was very sympathetic, and had tried to be unobtrusive, but I was still, inevitably, a part of the external threat. Besides, I was always associated with their own Dani enemies, among whom I had earlier lived for two years.

No sooner were the bamboo tubes passed out than they were collected again, and the boys were led back to the Sacred Place for a last meal. This time it was not cold fat and taro, but warm pork and sweet potatoes. Then each was given a bundle of firewood and sent home to present it to his mother. This last touch seemed strange, for it seemed to indicate that the boys had not been away at all, had not changed—they had just stepped out for some firewood. Certainly, this ceremony lacks the strong theme of antagonism toward women which has been reported from so many Papuan societies in New Guinea. Dani men and women live together calmly, with very little of the extremes of love and hate which punctuate our own relationships.

Now that the boys were home again, there was only one more major event—the wild pig feast. On May 16, two days after they had returned, I came to the compounds and found the men and boys gone. "They are hunting the wild pig," people explained. This was nonsense, I knew, because there were no wild pigs near the Grand Valley. I had never heard of any.

But the next day there was a final feast for the boys. Its ingredients were unique: crayfish, grasshoppers, mice and birds, bees and beehives, cockroaches, pandanus nuts, and one pig. The pig was indeed a wild pig, apparently, but I still do not know where and how they found it. The meal was a cacciatore, a sort of hunters' stew, of all the foods which the Dani hunt and gather, in contrast to the usual foods, cultivated sweet potato and taro, and domestic pig. Once, before they began their intensive sweet potato horticulture, the Dani had been foragers, living off the forest. Many traits in their culture today are survivals from this earlier, forgotten period, and now this final act of initiation took the boys back to the ancient culture.

The other themes of the initiation seem clearer. Even though only half the boys participate in it, it is a rite of passage for them. The time which the boys spend in the Sacred Place is a time of coldness: cold dew, cold food. When that time is over, they are thrown on a fire and fed hot food. This hot and cold symbolism is not expressed openly by the Dani, but I feel fairly confident in suggesting it. Others will want to take the symbolism further, thinking of the passages through the arches, of death and rebirth, of the red stripe as blood (perhaps as menstrual blood), of the firewood.

The Cutting of the Pig Skins

The event which makes the Pig Feast truly an Alliance ceremony is the Cutting of the Pig Skin. The weddings, after all, are many small events held simultaneously, and the initiation involves only some of the men and boys. But the Cutting of the Pig Skins brings the entire Alliance together for one climactic day every five or six years. The main purpose of this day is to settle the outstanding funerals: to placate for a last time the ghosts of people who have died or been killed since the last Pig Feast.

Early in the morning each compound prepares its pig skins—one for each of the major people who have died and are now to be commemorated. The skin of the pig, with its thick layer of fat, is steamed in one piece. Then, lashed to a frame which keeps the skin spread out, it is lifted onto a woman's back. There are few really unpleasant moments in Dani life, but for the women who have to carry the warm, dripping pig skins under the hot midday sun, this is one.

Through the late morning and early afternoon the skins were brought from all over the Alliance to Mabel's compound. This event marked the final confirmation of Mabel's ascendancy in the Alliance. Until this year it had been Gutelu's privilege to begin the Pig Feast; the major events had been held at Gutelu's compound, and were directed by Gutelu. Now Gutelu yielded with public grace to Mabel, and was a guest at Mabel's compound. Dani leadership is relatively informal and diffuse (see p. 71). The Big Men have no badges of rank and really very little power to command others— they lead by example and through consensus. But at moments like this, there was no question who was the leader of the Alliance. As the skins were brought into the courtyard, Mabel stood proud and alone, greeting people and directing his men in the laying out of the skins.

When the 175 skins were laid out, Mabel and his men ran back and forth along the lines, shouting to the ghosts to look and be satisfied. Then the skins were taken outside to a grassy field, where the men gathered in groups, each concerned with its own dead. By now the crowd was immense— certainly the largest gathering of Dani I have ever seen. There were thousands of people. In the center were the groups of men and pig skins; around them the women and children; even the brides, awkward in their new skirts, had managed to come and sat quietly among the trees at the edges of the groups.

Mabel himself began the Cutting of the Pig Skins. While two men held a skin up, he cut out pieces with a bamboo knife. As each piece was cut, he held it high in the air and shouted the name of the recipient. The first pieces went to the enemy leaders as a sign of peace and war, of respect and challenge. Then pieces went to those who had fought well and those who had lost relatives by war and by sickness. Soon the other Big Men began cutting their pig skins and shouting the names of recipients. When the major pieces had been distributed, the audience was fed: first the outsiders (missionaries, police, soldiers, schoolteachers, pilots, and anthropologists); then the people, men, women, and children. As the afternoon wore on, people smeared the last of the pig fat on their bodies and hair, and drifted off in small groups for home.

5 / Return to the Dani, 1988

Eighteen years passed before I was able to return to the Grand Valley. In October 1988, I took the Garuda Air flight from Jakarta to Los Angeles and interrupted it in Biak for a quick dash back to the Dani. From Biak I flew on to the airport at Lake Sentani, on the mainland, where General MacArthur had established his headquarters during the Second World War. Before flying up to the Highlands, it is necessary to make a side trip to the provincial capital, which was called "Hollandia" in 1961, but which was then changed by the Indonesians to "Kota Baru," then "Sukarnopura," and finally "Jayapura." Even by its fourth name, the city was still very recognizable. It is part shabby tropical port town and part feisty crossroads for all of eastern Indonesia. The people are lively and attractive, but they all seem to be young. This is no place for old men. The police permit to visit the Grand Valley was forthcoming, and early the next morning I took the Merpati flight into the Highlands, to Wamena. The coastal jungles were the same, and the central mountain ranges and even the Grand Valley itself looked hardly different. But then we landed in Wamena. What had been merely a handful of prefabricated metal houses beside the airstrip in 1961 is now a booming town of 5000 people. They have come from all over Irian and the rest of the Indonesian archipelago. It was positively cosmopolitan: schools, mosques, churches, a large market, a Chinese restaurant, a movie theater, photocopy shops, and even a restaurant run by the Minangkabau, the people of West Sumatra with whom I had just lived for two years. But there were few Dani: Some women sold vegetables in the market, some men wandered the roads offering tourist souvenirs, and some youths were baggage handlers in the airport terminal (which was built to resemble the domed men's houses). Also, some Dani were just sitting around the market or the airstrip listlessly watching things happen.

After looking around the town, I went to the bus station, and in my eagerness to get out of Wamena, I rented a whole minibus for the trip across the Grand Valley. In the old days the walk had taken two hours on a good day, or four hours when the paths were muddy or when no raft was handy to cross the Balim River. I had made the trip, usually alone, so many times that I knew every hill, every stream, every garden ditch along the way. Now the minibus took 15 minutes, speeding over the river on a steel bridge.

Wamena. Established as the administrative center for the Grand Valley in 1962, it has grown into a town of 5000 people.

My welcome at Wubakainma, where I had lived for so long, was intense. But it was at once warm and distant. Even after 18 years I recognized many people and they recognized me. Of course, I have been thinking and writing and speaking about them for all these years. For them the memories of the members of the old Harvard–Peabody Expedition were still fresh, and several people went through the list of names, asking me what had happened to each. I am sure that there has been a certain amount of mythologizing on both sides over the years. The new Catholic priest at Jibika, Father John Philip Saklil, told me that my name, Karoro (Karl has an un-Dani consonant cluster) is now a generic term for Westerner. Lexical immortality, I suppose. Since I had last been there I had learned Indonesian and Minangkabau, but my Dani had slipped far back into my brain. My old friends, with whom I had had so many long private conversations, had learned no Indonesian. The only way I could communicate was through younger people who had been to school and learned Indonesian. I was able to spend two days in the men's house at Wubakainma, and another two days at the Lauk Inn on the road by Gutelu's compound at Jibiga. My Dani slowly came back, but the people were less interested in talking with me than in looking at the photographs of themselves in the various books which I had brought for them. (No one reads English, but many of the people under 30 could work out the personal names and place names in the photo captions.)

The Dugum Neighborhood. View from the Southeast. The compounds of Wubakainma are at the right, hidden by the new shade trees. In the center, at the foot of the Dugum hill, is the auracaria grove of Homuak. It had been cut down for lumber in the 1960s, and is now growing back.

AFTER THE ETHNOGRAPHIC PRESENT

When we first arrived in the Dugum Neighborhood in 1961, we were seeing the Dani in a state which fairly approximated that conventional construct, "the ethnographic present." Soon, however, the Dutch government ended the warfare, and change was accelerated on many fronts. Even when I returned in 1968 and 1970 and lived at the mission station at Jibiga, I was thinking in terms of my 1961 experiences, the ethnographic present. And when I wrote the first chapters of this book in 1977, I was trying to evoke the 1961 period. If ever there was a case for using the ethnographic present, it was the Dani in 1961. But however convenient it is as a descriptive convention, it is misleading on theoretical grounds. It takes a single frozen slice of time out of the ongoing life of a culture and represents that culture by that slice. A holistic analysis will indeed show how various elements are interrelated at that moment, but still we are invited to understand that moment as the end product of history: Dani = 1961. There is an alternative strategy, which is to think of culture as process. By this strategy, we treat these ethnographic glimpses as data that record the ongoing transformations of a culture.

So, we can look at the Dani from one of two positions: If it is as the romantic end product, we take 1961 as the last moment of the full flowering of real Dani culture, and by doing so we recognize 1961 as the beginning of decay and dissolution; or if it is as process, we think of Dani culture as always in flux, and by doing so we recognize 1961 as the beginning of a particularly intense and rapid period of transformation. I admit to being of two minds on this question. As we shall see, I was somewhat downcast by my 1988 visit. My romantic side longed for the good old days when the Dani were truly themselves. But my processual side tried to understand the Dani of 1961 and the Dani of 1988 as part of the same continuity and rejected Golden Age thinking. (After all, how are we able to balance war deaths and finger mutilations against political and economic dependency?)

When writing the first part of this book in 1977, I did emphasize a 1961 prepacification picture of the Dani. Although I had spent nearly three years with the Dani, in fact only five months of that time was prepacification. And those months were of course my first months, when I understood the least about Dani culture. But writing in that mode was possible, and in my defense I should say that the reader will find numerous comments about changes before and after 1961. So I was able to record and analyze Dani culture according to both views.

But today it is no longer reasonable to treat the Dani as a pristine, isolated society. In the Grand Valley the influence of roads, schools, police, tourists, markets, and churches is so pervasive that no account can ignore the new mix. Jibiga, where I lived in 1968 and 1970 was then accessible only by airplane or by several hours of walking from Wamena across the valley floor. Now it is an easy and cheap bus trip, and the world floods in.

Many of my contemporaries in anthropology during the 1960s also did their dissertation research on relatively isolated societies like the Dani. Today most of those societies are no longer isolated and are in dire straights. They have been poisoned by chemical wastes; displaced by deforestation; ravaged by disease, drought, or some sort of low-intensity warfare. So far, the Dani are relatively lucky. They are being benignly overwhelmed and absorbed, but they are not being wiped out.

However, those Dani whom I knew best, in the Dugum Neighborhood, are in a particularly disadvantageous situation. The middle-aged and older people were too old to start school in the 1960s and so did not learn Indonesian. Because of this, they have had little opportunity to participate in the new order. But even the younger people are being left out, for the Neighborhood has become a backwater. The road passes through, but higher schools and markets are elsewhere. They can live at home and attend the first grades of Indonesian schools, but if they want to continue through secondary school they would have to move elsewhere—to Wamena or to Jibiga—and pay room and board. This takes money, however, and money is available only at markets, which are not to be found in the Neighborhood. One solution is to move away from the Neighborhood, but at the cost of breaking one's ties to land, sib, compound, and ritual groups. But, but, but. It is an old familiar story known around the world, and can only seem remarkable here because the dilemma has arisen so recently.

Jibiga. The large compound cluster at Jibiga where Gutelu, the leader of the Alliance, lives, and to where the Franciscan mission was first attracted. Now Jibiga has grown into an important center for churches, schools, and administration. In the middle background the road leads up the valley. The heavy bus, truck, and motor bike traffic has made airplanes unnecessary, and the airstrip, barely seen running diagonally across the middle of the photograph, has been abandoned.

CHANGE—THE NORMAL STATE

In the earlier chapters I discussed some of the changes which had already taken place before 1961, particularly the ending of cannibalism in the 1930s and the introduction of sweet potatoes and pigs much earlier. I also considered changes which had not taken hold in the Grand Valley but had already swept the Western Dani region. Some changes took place during the 1960s, like the cessation of chopping off little girls' fingers. The most dramatic change was pacification, but even by 1970 I could only guess at its ramifications.

Now we can talk about these changes with the benefit of greater perspective.

Nuts and Apples

When I first approached Um'ue's men's house in Wubakainma in 1988, the landscape was the same but different. That was not really surprising, for even in a few months in the Grand Valley one becomes sensitive to the ways in which large areas of garden land move from sweet potato fields to weeds to trees and back again to cultivated gardens. The first real shock was the profile of Wubakainma. Um'ue and his men had planted shade trees around the compound, and in 18 years the trees had grown tall. The change was not merely visual, for the sound of the wind through the new trees gave a whole new sense to the compounds.

Even more surprisingly, in the banana yards there were now mature pandanus trees bearing great red fruits. I could not recall ever having seen pandanus growing around the valley floor compounds. They belong in the mountains, and it takes a special expedition to harvest the fruit. It had never occurred to me that they might grow at the lower altitude. But obviously Um'ue had tried it, and was successful. Later I visited Um'ue's younger brother, Jege Asuk, the scapegrace. He had a new compound lying out toward the center of the valley, beside the road, where he was growing new crops like peanuts and apples. That summarized the difference between Um'ue and Jege Asuk. As long as I have known them, Um'ue has been the straight man, achieving much within traditional Dani norms, and Jege Asuk has been the adventurous innovator. (In April 1961 we were paying Dani one cowrie shell per load to carry our baggage up from the boat landing on the Aikhe River, and it was Jege Asuk who organized the first longshoremen's strike in the history of the Balim Valley. We went up to two cowries per load.)

Two brothers. Jege Asuk, the innovator, and his older brother Um'ue, the traditional Big Man (see photos on pp. 5, 7, and 73). Jege Asuk's compound has a bench and a house made of sawn planks, a new strain of pigs, and nearby he is growing peanuts and apples.

Women in the Men's House

I sat in Um'ue's men's house and presented copies of our various books to the people who were in them. Soon men and women and boys and girls were crowding around to gaze at photographs and to recall people and events. The pictures of warfare were especially fascinating, for no one under their mid-30s had any real memory of it. Meanwhile, as I sat back and looked at the crowd, I was startled and was barely able to repress the urge to admonish them: "Don't you know that it is *wusa* for women to enter a men's house?"

And indeed, what had happened to weaken the ban on women here in the men's house? Five kilometers away the Christian churches at Jibiga were growing, but not many people from the Dugum Neighborhood had yet converted. And in any case I doubt if the rules of *wusa,* or taboo, would be seen by the Dani as directly opposed to Christianity. I think the explanation is that Dani religious practices wax and wane in their intensity in response to stresses of war, death, and accidents. Now that these stresses are minimal, concerns with *wusa* have declined, and as it happens, other possible problems such as alcoholism have not risen. But in any case, as the next example suggests, it seems unlikely that any sort of feminist movement has opened the men's houses to Dani women.

Fingers and Shovels: Division of Labor

In the old days, almost all women were missing several fingers which had been sacrificed in funeral ceremonies. Also, women used the slender digging sticks for weeding and harvesting, but only the men used the larger, heavier digging sticks which could break and turn sod. It seemed a reasonable guess that this division of labor was to some extent determined by the difficulties which women would have had trying to wield the heavy digging sticks with their mutilated hands.

But in the mid-1960s the Dani stopped chopping off girls' fingers (see p. 133). When I returned in 1968 and 1970, the younger girls all had intact fingers. And of course by 1988 these girls had become the women who form the bulk of the female work force today.

As iron tools became available, Dani slowly adopted knives, bush knives, and axes. But even in 1970 steel-bladed shovels were not much desired and were rarely used. By 1988, however, shovels had become common, and were hafted on handles which are about the size of the old women's digging sticks.

And in the Dugum Neighborhood the division of labor has shifted. Women now help out with the heavy first tasks of the garden, hefting the new efficient shovels with their unmutilated hands.

As far as I could tell in 1988, the men have not taken on more tasks, which results in one of the ironies of modernization: The Dani women, no longer subject to losing their fingers as sacrifices to the ghosts, take on a larger share of the horticultural labor. And the men, relieved of these and many other duties, have yet more time to sit and talk.

Diminishing Men's Spheres

Except in a few isolated hilly corners of the Grand Valley, warfare has long since ended. Thus, the Dani no longer have to bear the tremendous costs in time and resources which had been invested in weapons, in defensive structures and guard duties, and in actual warfare and its ceremonial aftermaths, not to mention the costs of war injuries and deaths. The same Indonesian police and civilian officials who enforce pacification have also taken over the major activities of Dani political institutions. Disputes are now resolved by policemen, who are usually non-Dani, rather than by the Big Men of the area. And Christian missionaries, who had little apparent success in the Grand Valley during the 1950s and 1960s, have seen a dramatic change in their influence. In the late 1960s the Franciscan mission at Jiwiga would attract at most a few dozen Dani to the Sunday services. By 1988 an Indonesian pastor is in place, and the new sanctuary is regularly jammed with hundreds of Dani each Sunday. Not all of them are converts, though; many simply drop by on their way to the Sunday market, which is located at the edge of the mission station. Even so, more are moving closer to Christianity, and as they do so they are moving farther from their traditional religious practices.

In all these ways the role of Dani men has been diminished: in horticulture, in warfare and other political activities, and in religion. For these men, and especially for the older men who have not learned Indonesian, there is more time to simply sit and talk. For the younger men, though, who

Conflict resolution. At the Jibiga police post a policeman hears a complaint brought by some Dani men from a nearby compound.

Gutelu at the Jibiga market. Every Sunday people gather at Jibiga for the market. The variety of foods which they offer is not much different from what they grew in 1961. With the cash which they earn, they buy cloth, soap, flashlights, batteries, knives, and the like. Gutelu, the older leader, wanders the market alone.

Wejak. One of the main figures in Robert Gardner's film Dead Birds.

have embraced some of the new ways, there are few chances to ride the new waves. The Grand Valley is flooded with Indonesians from elsewhere who have moved into the small entrepreneurial roles like bus driving and tourist services. And most of the tourists, who would otherwise generate a lot of local business, seem to be independent trekers with backpacks who head for the most isolated Dani compounds and who pride themselves in their self-sufficiency. Pua, the young boy in Robert Gardner's film *Dead Birds,* had tried to run a small guest house for tourists, but it had little success. In 1988 it was closed, and Pua was no longer living in the Grand Valley. All this translates into no jobs for the Dani except at the very lowest levels. Even the comparatively innovative Jege Asuk seems to be growing his peanuts and apples as if they were sweet potatoes and bananas. He has not broken out of the traditional Dani horticultural pattern by very much.

Political Disorganization

Compared with the political system of other groups in the New Guinea Highlands, the Grand Valley Dani political system was unusually complex. In most other parts of the Highlands, even in the Western Dani region, the largest sociopolitical groups were like the Grand Valley confederations, with a few hundred to a thousand people. Kin groups like sibs and moieties were spread wider than the confederations, but they are more symbolic than effective units of social action. However, in the Grand Valley these confederations were combined into larger groups of up to 5000 people. Warfare and the major religious activities were organized at the alliance level.

But now, two factors have combined to diminish the importance of the alliance. Pacification did away with warfare, which was the main ongoing function of the alliance. And in the interests of administrative convenience, the Indonesian government has been emphasizing the smaller units, the confederations, and singling out confederation-level leaders. In the process, of course, this reduces the importance of the alliance-level leadership. The traditional Big Men, whose power derived from influence and persuasion, are being turned into Chiefs, with power now being derived from the Indonesian state and contained at the confederation level.

The poignant symbol of this change was Gutelu himself. In the early 1960s he was one of the greatest and canniest of all Grand Valley Big Men. By the end of the decade he was more of an elder statesman of the Alliance, and the effective leadership had shifted to the younger man, Mabel. But Gutelu had an aura. He had been to the coast, he had met President Sukarno, and as a sign of his great involvement in *wusa,* or magical power, he was the only adult Dani male who refused to smoke tobacco. In 1988, although he was mentally still sharp and sly, he had become old and stooped. He wandered around the area cadging cigarettes from outsiders.

Gutelu. Once the leader of the Alliance. (see photograph on p. 147)

He has given his name to the whole area, and it is painted on the sides of the minibuses which ply the road. Even so, Gutelu himself must pay his fare like anyone else. The confederations are robust, the alliance-level organization is withering, and Gutelu is irrelevant.

Power vs. Egalitarianism: The Fate of Polygyny

Turn to page 83. There you will find one of my predictions written in 1977: With pacification, war deaths would cease, and the deficit of males in the population pyramid would no longer exist. With an increase in the eligible male population, polygyny could not continue without incurring a great social cost. Either monogamy would emerge as the Dani pattern, or if polygyny did persist, some men would be without wives. My prediction was that Dani egalitarianism would result in each youth getting married, and none would be able to marry extra wives at the expense of their fellows.

It is still perhaps too early to be sure, and my data are far from adequate. But it looks as if my prediction was wrong. There are still young men with multiple wives. And there are some, like Wamasue (pictured as a baby in the photograph on page 10) who are nearing 30 and who are still not married. His case is not really surprising. His father is dead and he lives with his aged mother as a poor relative in the compound of Um'ue. He seems to have little access to the goods necessary for the wedding

Wamasue. A bachelor. (see photograph of him as a child, p. 10)

exchanges. He cannot compete with those of his peers whose fathers and uncles can easily provide them with pigs and shells. I am a bit hesitant to interpret too much on the basis of so little. But it does look as if several changing factors have kept Wamasue a bachelor: the larger number of living males, the weakening of kinship ties and support, the greater importance of material goods, and an egalitarian ethic which is weaker than I had thought earlier. The first three factors are relatively amenable to measurement. The egalitation factor is very elusive, and raises the interesting questions: To what extent might I have over estimated it in the 1960s? To what extent is such a pattern ephemeral, and easily subject to change?

Cultural Awareness

One of the most fascinating changes is the growth of a new mind set, especially the developing awareness of the multicultural nature of the world. In 1961 no Dani in the Dugum Neighborhood was bilingual. They understood us outsiders only as some strange variation of themselves. No one ever believed that I, with all my obvious wealth, did not have many pigs and wives. A constant problem of fieldwork in those days was their total disinterest in the idea of culture, their own as well as ours. And thus, they had a total lack of understanding about what I was trying to accomplish. I have tried to explain it in terms of a low level of intellectualism. But it always puzzled me (and hampered my research) that even the smartest and most knowledgeable Dani should be so nonintrospective.

This is changing drastically as the younger Dani—those born in the 1960s and later—have become comfortably bilingual in Dani and Indonesian, are moving back and forth from the compounds to the town of Wamena, buying, selling, and reading. They are the ones who are forging the new mix which is the Dani culture today, a Dani–Indonesian–Christian culture. It is their parents and grandparents, who are still monolingual and who are still only peripherally Indonesian, who will continue to live in a diminished ethnographic present.

NEW FINDINGS AND OLD

The single most important ethnographic finding of my earlier work on the Dani was surely the five-year postpartum sexual abstinence pattern (see pp. 84–87). It is also the most controversial finding, and few other scholars know quite what to make of it. Unfortunately, I had no opportunity in those very public and hectic days in 1988 to get more information about Dani sexuality.

The single greatest omission in my earlier work turns out to be (so far) the ceremony called *ima wusan,* an incest purification rite.

In 1988, when I visited the Franciscan mission in Wamena, Father Frans Lieshout showed me a monograph by John van de Pavert (1986) which described the *ima wusan.* It is a ceremony of repair, used when a man and a woman of the same moiety have had sex together, thus committing incest (see p. 83). In this ceremony they publically confess their sin, are absolved and purified, and then reincorporated into normal society.

I have to admit that at first I was skeptical. How could I have missed such a ceremony in all the time that I had spent with the Dani? But of course, the fact was that Dani rarely announced a ceremony to me in advance. If I stumbled on it, fine. Then I would be welcome to watch, take notes and photographs, and ask people about it afterward. But no one would bother to seek me out and direct me to it. I wonder what I would have understood about the great Pig Feast (pp. 138–152) if I had not heard about it in some detail from the Dutch. It was not until the end of my third year of fieldwork that I actually saw it. By then I had used the Dutch descriptions as guides to work out details with informants. But what if I had been totally ignorant of it? Could I possibly have put together any reasonable picture of it on the basis of the odd references which popped up in other conversations and interviews? I doubt it.

There was a hint in Jan Broekhuijse's dissertation (1967:21), but I missed its significance. Father Jules Camps actually filmed the ceremony near Jibiga in December 1971, but I had been gone more than a year by then.

My first reaction on hearing that Roman Catholic priests had discovered a Dani ceremony of confession and absolution was one of great wariness. It was too neat. Recently (1988), I wrote about "The Rashomon Effect," the notion that different ethnographers may construct quite different pictures of societies for a variety of reasons, as the result of a variety of influences which include their own personal philosophies. Would it be possible that the priests, looking at the Dani through their own confessional tradition, would recognize a confessional rite that I, a nonconfessional Protestant, would have been blinded to? I am confident that if I had actually stumbled onto the ceremony, I would not have ignored it. But it is quite possible that my own mind set hindered me from recognizing clues when I did come across them. (And, after all, even the Catholics took nearly two decades to find it.) My skepticism was dispelled (and my self-annoyance increased) when I asked Um'ue and others about *ima wusan* in 1988. They quite matter-of-factly acknowledged it.

What next for the Dani? Stay tuned. Their story will continue to unfold.

Appendix / Three Films on the Grand Valley Dani

Dead Birds (1963)   (83 minutes)

Credits: A film by Robert Gardner. Photography, Editing, Writing: Robert Gardner; Sound Recording: Michael Rockefeller; Sound Editing: Jairus Lincoln; Photographic Assistant: Karl G. Heider; Titles: Peter Chermayeff; Advisers: Jan Broekhuijse and Peter Matthiessen. This film was produced by the Film Study Center of the Peabody Museum at Harvard University with help from the former Netherlands New Guinea Government and the National Science Foundation.

Distribution: Phoenix Films, Inc. 470 Park Avenue South, New York, NY 10016; CRM/McGraw-Hill Films, Del Mar, CA 92014; Pennsylvania State University Audio-Visual Services, University Park, PA 16802; University of California Extension Media Center, 2223 Fulton St., Berkeley, CA 94720

Dead Birds was shot and recorded during the period April–August 1961 in the Grand Valley of the Balim, and it was edited during the next 18 months in the Film Study Center at Harvard. Something of the making of the film is described in Chapter 1; there are more details in my book *Ethnographic Film* (1976) and in a study guide which I prepared for the film (1972). Robert Gardner, the filmmaker, has described his ideas about the film in two essays (1971 and 1972).

It is good to think for a moment about the differences between film and book. This book has been able to touch on most aspects of Dani life in 160 pages, which contain about 90,000 words, 36 photographs, and 19 maps, tables, and diagrams. In the 83 minutes of *Dead Birds,* there are nearly 62,000 photographic frames which are projected at 24 frames each second, and these frames are organized in about 628 different shots. The spoken narration consists of about 5700 words, or the equivalent of about eight pages of text. The photographs provide countless more contextualizing details than any printed page can, but photographs cannot draw attention to details the way that words can. So on the other hand, there is much more raw information in the film than in the book; on the other hand, the film explicitly emphasizes only a few things. Thus, one can view the film casually for a few major impressions, but as one sees the film a second and third time, one can learn more and more from it.

We learn early how to get information from books, but we are accustomed to looking at films only for entertainment. The great challenge of using ethnographic film for learning about another culture lies in this: how one can learn to see, and, in seeing, learn.

It may be good to call attention to several main themes, or threads of information, which run through the film. The following is meant to be a guide to viewing the film, not a synopsis of the plot:

1. The Dani environment. From the opening shots which sweep across the Dugum Neighborhood, Gardner shows Dani houses, compounds, paths, fields, and forests in relationship to each other.

2. Dani people. There are hundreds of Dani in the film, and we can see how they look, how they dress, and how they move.

3. Dani artifacts and how they are used.

4. Dani warfare or at least the battles of the ritual phase of Dani warfare (see the discussion on pp. 97–100). Gardner has carefully set warfare in its cultural context, but when people see *Dead Birds* for the first time, they tend to remember the scenes of fighting and not the context.

5. Salt production. Intercut with the scenes of men at war are scenes of women preparing salt.

6. Sweet potato horticulture appears mainly as background throughout the film.

7. Ritual events are shown frequently enough to give a good idea of the tone of Dani ritual. However, because this theme is fundamentally so abstract and symbolic, it is one of the hardest to handle through photographs alone, and the explanatory narration (as well as Chapters 3 and 4 of this study) becomes essential at these moments.

8. Finger mutilation of girls is foreshadowed by shots of women with their mutilated hands. Then at the funeral we see the girls who have just lost fingers, their hands bandaged and their faces showing the dull shock. The film does not put this mutilation sufficiently into context so that audiences can understand it, and therefore those scenes too often appall American audiences. But this reaction is not at all surprising, and cannot be considered a fault of the film for, as I argue on pages 133–136, finger mutilation of the girls is incompatible with the rest of Dani culture.

9. Two Dani emerge especially clearly as individuals: Wejak, the warrior, and Pua, the little swineherd. Lakha, one of Wejak's wives, is the only woman seen often enough for one to get a sense of her as a real person. Many other Dani, especially those who lived near us in the Dugum Neighborhood, appear again and again in the film, and some viewers will begin to recognize them. Wejak and Pua are not, of course, fully typical of all Dani men and all Dani boys. But Gardner does use them to personalize the Dani, saying, in effect, "This is how a Dani man and a Dani boy were."

10. The theme of Man-as-Bird (see pp. 126–127). In his first version of *Dead Birds,* which was some 40 minutes longer than this one, Gardner used this symbolic identification between man and bird—so basic to Dani thought—much more extensively, and the narration made it much more

explicit. In the present version much of the visual allusion to it remains, but the narration hardly refers to the symbol except in the opening lines (which are often lost because audiences are not prepared for such important information so early). Those opening lines are:

> There is a fable told by mountain people living in the ancient highlands of New Guinea about a race between a snake and a bird. It tells of a contest which decided if men would be like birds and die, or be like snakes which shed their skins and have eternal life. The bird won and from time to time, all men, like birds, must die (Gardner 1963).

11. Gardner's own philosophy vis-à-vis the Dani. More than most anthropologists or filmmakers (and he is both), Gardner has been very explicit about his own views of the Dani. We can see this in the film as well as in various essays (e.g., Gardner and Heider 1969, Gardner 1971, 1972). This openness makes it easy to examine and to criticize Gardner's approach. It is well summed up by the following words:

> A Dani is a plumed warrior in his most desirous state. What I have done is to acknowledge this indubitable fact and be glad for its wry, perhaps ironic, implications. I saw the Dani people, feathered and fluttering men and women, as enjoying the fate of all men and women. They dressed their lives with plumage, but faced as certain death as the rest of us drabber souls. The film attempts to say something about how we all, as humans, meet our animal fate (Gardner 1972:35).

Finally, a word about the artifice of the filmmaking. Gardner was with the Dani for about five months, and filmed only a tiny fraction of the reality going on around him 24 hours a day. When he returned to his lab, he selected for use in the final edited film only about one foot of film for every 15 which he had shot; so there was a tremendous amount of choice going on. In some cases footage shot in different places was edited altogether—the battle sequences, for example, give a true picture of "Dani battle" but not an accurate account of any one particular battle. The major events in the film did happen in the sequence shown (except that the women's trip to the brine pool was not shot during a battle). Some battles, raids, deaths, funerals were omitted (compare the film with the chronology on pp. 97–100). A few of the shots could be said to be directed—for example the cut-away shots of Pua watching his pigs, when Gardner would move in close to Pua and tell him to look at pigs, not the camera. But we did not stage, direct, request, or pay for major events like battles or rituals (see p. 19).

Dani Sweet Potatoes (1974)   (19 minutes)
Dani Houses (1974)   (16 minutes)

Credits: Photographed, Edited, and Narrated by Karl G. Heider with sponsorship from the Social Studies Curriculum of Educational Development Center under a grant from the National Science Foundation.

Distribution: University of California Extension Media Center; 2223 Fulton Street, Berkeley, CA 94720; Pennsylvania State University Audio-Visual Services, University Park, PA 16802.

In 1963, during my second trip to the Dani, I shot footage on technology. The project was financed by a curriculum development program which wanted to have footage on digging-stick horticulture, but in the end that particular unit never was realized. I bought work prints of the footage and edited it into two sequences, each nearly an hour long. One was on house building and the other on sweet potato horticulture. Then for several years I showed these rough-cut films to various audiences, doing a live narration myself. With the help of the audience reactions I slow cut the length of the films and adapted the narration to answer questions which the footage raised. But I was busy with other Dani research, and did not have access to any editing facilities, so the rough cuts remained rough. Finally, in the summer of 1972 in Santa Fe, New Mexico, Carroll Williams gave me instruction and the use of his equipment, and I was able to do the narrations and finish the films. By then the footage had been boiled down to an essential 16 and 19 minutes. (Only other filmmakers can understand how painful it is to discard footage, but they also understand how necessary it is.)

Dani Sweet Potatoes has a major theme and a minor theme. The film focuses on the sequence of sweet potato horticulture in the valley floor gardens (which is described on pp. 40–44). I shot most of this footage while following Um'ue's family. Um'ue himself clears a garden area; one of his wives plants the sweet potatoes and then, with her two-year-old daughter, harvests the tubers. The memorial feast at the end of the film, when the sweet potatoes are cooked, is held in Um'ue's compound at Wubakainma. A secondary or background theme is the behavior of small children, particularly the two-year-old Hagigake.

In *Dani Houses* we follow the construction of a long house and a round house.

Both of these films, perhaps because they were filmed of everyday activities during peacetime by an anthropologist who had been studying and living with them for two years, reflect more of the calm routine pattern of Dani culture than does *Dead Birds,* which was shot in our first exciting months of exploration with the Dani.

Bibliography

ARCHBOLD, RICHARD. 1941 "Unknown New Guinea." *National Geographic* 79(3):315–344.

BROEKHUIJSE, J. TH. 1967 *De Wiligiman-Dani.* Tilburgh: H. Gianotten N.V.

BROMLEY, H. MYRON. 1962 "The function of fighting in Grand Valley Dani Society." *Working Papers in Dani Ethnology,* No. 1. Bureau of Native Affairs, Hollandia-Kota Baru.

———. 1972 "The Grammar of Lower Grand Valley Dani in Discourse Perspective." Unpublished Ph.D. dissertation, Department of Anthropology, Yale University.

BROOKFIELD, H. C. 1971 *Melanesia: A Geographical Interpretation of an Island World.* London: Methuen & Co.

BROWN, PAULA, and AARON PODOLEFSKY. 1976 "Population Density, Agricultural Intensity, Land Tenure, and Group Size in the New Guinea Highlands." *Ethnology* 15(3):211–238.

EKMAN, PAUL. 1972 "Universals and Cultural Differences in Facial Expressions of Emotion," in *Nebraska Symposium on Motivation, 1971.* Lincoln: University of Nebraska Press, pp. 207–283.

GARDNER, ROBERT G. 1963 *Dead Birds,* a film produced by the Film Study Center, Peabody Museum, Harvard University. New York: Contemporary Films, Inc., distributor.

———. 1971 "A Chronicle of the Human Experience: Dead Birds," in Lewis Jacobs, ed., *The Documentary Experience: From Nanook to Woodstock.* New York: Hopkinson and Blake, pp. 430–436.

———. 1972 "On the Making of Dead Birds," pp. 31–35 in Heider, 1972a.

———, and KARL G. HEIDER. 1969 *Gardens of War: Life and Death in the New Guinea Stone Age.* New York: Random House.

GERBRANDS, ADRIAN A., ed. 1967 *The Asmat of New Guinea: The Journal of Michael Clark Rockefeller.* New York: The Museum of Primitive Art.

GLASSE, ROBERT M. 1968 *Huli of Papua. A Cognatic Descent System.* Cahiers de l'Homme, n.s. VIII. Paris: Mouton & Co.

GOLSON, JACK. 1977 "No Room at the Top: Agricultural Intensification in the New Guinea Highlands," in J. Allen, J. Golson, and R. Jones, eds., *Sunda and Sahul: Prehistoric Studies in Southeast Asia, Melanesia and Australia.* London: Academic Press, pp. 601–638.

HEIDER, KARL G. 1967a "Speculative Functionalism: Archaic Elements in New Guinea Dani Culture," *Anthropos* 62:833–840.

———. 1967b "Archaeological Assumptions and Ethnographical Facts: A Cautionary Tale from New Guinea," *Southwestern Journal of Anthropology* 23 (1):52–64.

———. 1969a "Sweet Potato Notes and Lexical Queries," Kroeber Anthropological Society Papers, 41:78–86.

———. 1969b "Attributes and Categories in the Study of Material Culture: New Guinea Dani Attire" *Man* 4(3):379–391.

———. 1970 *The Dugum Dani: A Papuan Culture in the Highlands of West New Guinea.* Chicago: Aldine.

———. 1972a *The Dani of West Irian: An Ethnographic Companion to the Film Dead Birds.* New York: Warner Modular Publications Inc.

———. 1972b "The Grand Valley Dani Pig Feast: A Ritual of Passage and Intensification." *Oceania* 42(3):T69–197.

———. 1974a *Dani Sweet Potatoes,* a film distributed by the University of California Extension Media Center, Berkeley.

———. 1974b *Dani Houses,* a film distributed by the University of California Extension Media Center, Berkeley.

———. 1975a "What Do People Do? Dani Auto-ethnography." *Journal of Anthropological Research* 31(1):3–17.

———. 1975b "Societal Intensification and Cultural Stress as Causal Factors in the Innovation and Conservatism of Two Dani Cultures." *Oceania* 46(1):53–67.

———. 1976a "Dani Children's Development of Competency in Social Structural Concepts, *Ethnology* 15(3):47–62.

———. 1976b "Dani Sexuality: A Low Energy System," *Man.*

———. 1976c *Ethnographic Film.* Austin: University of Texas Press.

———. 1977 "From Javanese to Dani: The Translation of a Game." In *Studies in the Anthropology of Play: Papers in Memory of B. Allan Tindall,* Phillips Stevens, Jr., ed. Proceedings of the 2d Annual Meeting of the Association for the Anthropological Study of Play.

———. 1978 "Accounting for Variation: A Non-Formal Analysis of Grand Valley Kinship Terms," *Journal of Anthropological Research,* 34.2:219–262.

———, ms. *Dani Patterns: A Psychological Ethnography of a New Guinea Culture.*

HEIDER, KARL G. 1988 "The Rashomon Effect: When Ethnographers Disagree." *American Anthropologist* 90(1):73–81.

HITT, RUSSELL T. 1962 *Cannibal Valley.* New York: Harper & Row.

KOCH, KLAUS-FRIEDRICH. 1970 "Cannibalistic Revenge in Jalé Society." *Natural History* 79(2):40–51.

———. 1974 *War and Peace in Jalémo: The Management of Conflict in Highland New Guinea.* Cambridge: Harvard University Press.

LOMAX, ALAN. 1962 "Song Structure and Social Structure." *Ethnology* 1:425–451.

MATTHIESSEN, PETER. 1962 *Under the Mountain Wall: A Chronicle of Two Seasons in the Stone Age.* New York: Viking.

O'BRIEN, DENISE, and ANTON PLOEG. 1964 "Acculturation Movements among the Western Dani," *American Anthropologist* 66(4.2):281–292.

POSPISIL, LEOPOLD. 1958 *Kapauku Papuans and Their Law.* New Haven: Yale University Publications in Anthropology, 54.

———. 1963 *Kapauka Papuan Economy.* New Haven: Yale University Publications in Anthropology, 67.

RAPPAPORT, ROY A. 1967 *Pigs for the Ancestors: Ritual in the Ecology of a New Guinea People.* New Haven: Yale University Press.

ROBERTS, JOHN M., MALCOLM J. ARTH, and ROBERT R. BUSH. 1959 "Games in Culture," *American Anthropologist* 61(4):597–605.

SAHLINS, MARSHALL. 1963 "Poor Man, Rich Man, Big-Man, Chief: Political Types in Melanesia and Polynesia." *Comparative Studies in Society and History* 5(3):285–303.

VAN DE PAVERT, JOHN. 1986 "Ima Wusan." A Purification Ritual Among the Dani of West New Guinea. *UNITAS* 59(1), Manila: University of Santo Tomas.

VAN DER STAP. P. A. M. 1966 *Outline of Dani Morphology. Verhandeligen van het Koninklijk Instituut voor Taal-, Land- en Volkenkunde.* Deel 48. 's-Gravenhage: Martinus Nijhoff.

VAYDA, A. P., and R. A. RAPPAPORT. 1968 "Ecology, Cultural and Noncultural," in J. A. Clifton, ed., *Introduction to Cultural Anthropology.* Boston: Houghton-Mifflin, pp. 477–497.

WHITE, J. PETER, 1972 *Ol Tumbuna: Archaelogical excavations in the Eastern Central Highlands, Papua New Guinea.* Terra Australis 2. Canberra: Department of Prehistory, Research School of Pacific Studies, The Australian National University.

Index